D1827197

Electoral Politics in Punjab

This book examines electoral politics in the state of Punjab, India as it has evolved since the colonial period. It underlines the emergence of the state as a singular unit for electoral analysis in the last three decades.

This book:

- Charts the common trends and developments that have dominated politics in Punjab, and those that continue to play an important role in the government of the state;
- Examines state parties and their leadership in the context of party alliances, campaigns and electoral verdicts;
- Presents a comparative study of the assembly and Lok Sabha elections held in the state after reorganisation in 1966 with the objective of highlighting differences in electoral issues taken up by the parties.

An important intervention in the study of state-level politics in India, this book will be of great interest to students and researchers of politics, especially comparative politics and political institutions, political sociology and social anthropology, and South Asian studies.

Ashutosh Kumar is Professor at the Department of Political Science, Panjab University, Chandigarh, India. He has been associated with the Lokniti Network, CSDS, Delhi, India as state coordinator for Punjab. He was previously visiting faculty at the University of Tampere, Finland and Maison des Sciences de l'Homme, Paris, France. His research centers around state politics, with a focus on the issues related to elections, identities, and development. He is the editor of *Rethinking State Politics in India* (2011) and co-editor of *Globalisation and Politics of Identity in India* (2008) and *How India Votes: A State-by-state Look* (2019). He has also published extensively in various international journals such as *India Review*, *EPW*, *South Asia Research*, *Japanese Journal of Political Science*, *Asian Ethnicity*, *International Journal of Punjab Studies*, *Journal of Sikh & Punjab Studies*, *and Journal of Asian and African Studies*, among others.

Electoral Politics in Punjab

Factors and Phases

Ashutosh Kumar

Routledge
Taylor & Francis Group

LONDON AND NEW YORK

First published 2020
by Routledge
2 Park Square, Milton Park, Abingdon, Oxon OX14 4RN

and by Routledge
52 Vanderbilt Avenue, New York, NY 10017

Routledge is an imprint of the Taylor & Francis Group, an informa business

British Library Cataloguing-in-Publication Data
A catalogue record for this book is available from the British Library

Library of Congress Cataloging-in-Publication Data
Names: Kumar, Ashutosh, 1963– author.
Title: Electoral politics in Punjab : factors and phases / Ashutosh
    Kumar.
Description: Abingdon, Oxon ; New York, NY : Routledge, 2020. |
    Includes bibliographical references and index.
Identifiers: LCCN 2019044281 (print) | LCCN 2019044282 (ebook)
Subjects: LCSH: Elections—India—Punjab. | Political campaigns—
    India—Punjab. | Political parties—India—Punjab. | Punjab
    (India)—Politics and government.
Classification: LCC JQ578 .K86 2020 (print) | LCC JQ578 (ebook) |
    DDC 324.954/552—dc23
LC record available at https://lccn.loc.gov/2019044281
LC ebook record available at https://lccn.loc.gov/2019044282

ISBN: 978-1-138-54481-9 (hbk)
ISBN: 978-1-003-01128-6 (ebk)

Typeset in Sabon
by Apex CoVantage, LLC

Contents

Acknowledgements

The author wishes to thank the CSDS-Lokniti team led by the centre's director Sanjay Kumar and consisting of Vibha Atri, Jyoti Mishra, Shreyas Sardesai, and Himanshu Bhattacharya for making available the post-poll surveys data concerning Punjab. Thanks also go to the fellow Lokniti network members from universities/research centres from across India, especially to Jagrup Singh Sekhon with whom I have collaborated in conducting the surveys, and also have co-authored a couple of papers based on the survey data which are cited in the volume. I am also thankful to the students of Panjab University who have participated in the election surveys since the 2002 Assembly elections, going into the field and not only collecting the data but also coming out with insights. I am beholden to my present and former colleagues in the Department of Political Science, Panjab University and University of Jammu for most fruitful academic comradeship. Malkit Singh and Hardeep Kaur, researchers in the department, deserve special mention as they supervised these post-poll surveys. The monograph draws very extensively from the earlier published works in academic journals, national newspapers and book chapters on the subject by the author, cited in the text.

1 Framing state-level electoral politics

An introduction

India for a long time has been hailed worldwide for being a successful democracy. Its success, however, is being viewed and judged primarily in its minimalist form, encompassing nothing but a multiparty system, periodically held free elections, high levels of participation, and contestation that result in the peaceful and regular transfers of political power on a periodic basis. As a 'new' democracy, India has an uninterrupted history of holding free elections over more than seven decades now (even the emergency imposed in the mid-seventies did not disturb this, it only delayed it for a year).[1] In its seven-decades old democratic career, the country has been witness to 17 Lok Sabha elections and nearly 400 Assembly elections, not to mention the countless local bodies' elections which have got their own salience after the seventy-third and seventy-fourth constitutional amendment (Kumar, 2019c, p. 1).[2]

India has become a far more representative democracy in recent decades, as demonstrated by increased level of participation and representation. The impressive size and scale of social and cultural identities along the regional lines have contributed to the presence of political parties of different hues, each having distinct claims to represent these identities. It is not only the sheer number of parties but also the variety of these parties in terms of their ideologies, the social and spatial support base that easily makes Indian democracy akin to 'an electoral laboratory'. Adam Ziegfeld (2016) considers India ideal for studying party systems in comparative mode on two grounds: First, India is comparable to western democracies for having a 'lengthy democratic history and record of free and fair elections' with its many parties, which are 'short-lived, non-ideological, highly personalistic, and poorly organised', also compares with the party systems of the 'new' democracies. Second, India also presents an 'unparalleled setting' to study the 'puzzling variation' in the success of regional/state level parties as they 'vary in their age, ideological orientation, and support bases' (Ziegfeld, 2016, p. 6).

What has also impressed the political analysts is the sheer scale[3] at which the people's participation takes place in India's elections involving so many candidates from diverse social and economic backgrounds in the fray. India's electorates constitute one-sixth of the global electorates. Arguably, India qualifies to be considered ideal for studying an impressive range of elections-related issues like the electorates' attitudes and behaviour, manifestos and campaigns, and leadership models that these elections and contending parties throw up. Indian voters stand out for not only that the voters from the marginal social and economic background vote in almost equal percentage than the privileged voters unlike the western democracies but also there has been a sharp decrease in the gender gap and an increase in women turnout in both the Lok Sabha and Assembly elections, especially since 2002, as per the election commission of India data (Kumar and Gupta, 2015, p. 8). Indian 'exceptionalism' also is reflected in the voting behaviour of the Indian voters as almost half of them firm up their voting choices even before the commencement of the election campaign thus underlining their political attentiveness (CSDS-Lokniti national election studies data). This is unlike the western democracies where 'time of vote choice' data reveal that an increasing number of voters are making their voting choices only after the start of the election campaign (Sardesai and Mishra, 2017, p. 84).

Speaking of leadership, India has had 'many more political leaders than other countries—leaders who have won and lost elections, run and mis-run governments, and exercised the political imagination of their constituents in myriad other ways' (Guha, 2010, p. 288).[4] The list includes not only the national but also the other leaders who in their political life remained confined to a particular state or a sub-region within a state and yet were able to play a significant role at the national level (Kumar, 2019c, p. 265).[5]

Arguably, elections form the 'central institution' of India's democracy (Lama-Rewal, 2009, p. 2). The centrality argument gets credence when one thinks in procedural/ institutional terms. At a time when there is a perceptible trust deficit even for the constitutional bodies and functionaries (not to mention the statutory bodies), the Election Commission of India (ECI) has done fairly well to retain the confidence of the citizens. The ECI has been globally recognised for holding 'free and fair' elections. Also, it has pushed successfully for electoral reforms (Kumar, 2019c).

Deepening trust deficit in formal democratic institutions along with lack of effective 'non-electoral' democratic procedures, forums, and peoples' movements on the ground[6] persuade some political analysts to even suggest that the meaning of democracy in India is getting 'menacingly narrowed to signify only elections', as elections not only 'legitimise and authorise the democratic rule but does much more than this' (Khilnani, 1997, p. 193; Palshikar, 2013, p. 165).[7] Connected to almost every aspect of the democratic polity in a significant way, elections in India carry 'the entire society's aspirations to control its opportunities' to the extent that as the 'sole bridge between state and society, they have come to stand for democracy itself' (Khilnani, 1997, p. 58).[8]

What has brought the institution of elections still closer to the citizens in the last three decades is the introduction of local bodies' elections as a result of 73rd and 74th constitutional amendments. It has added yet another level of competitive electoral system extending it effectively to the grass-roots level, making it much more inclusive and competitive.[9] Arguably, local elections now held every five years in every state under the supervision have further strengthened and provided legitimacy to the basic framework of India's democratic regime (Kumar, 2019c).[10]

Not surprisingly, then, the study of elections,[11] electoral system and electoral politics[12] along with the study of parties and party system holds great significance[13] in the study of Indian politics. Significant social and political upheavals taking place in India, having their impact over the electoral arena, especially since the momentous 1990s, has been of great interest to the analysts (Kumar, 2019c).[14]

Given the vibrancy of electoral democracy in India, greater academic focus has been on the role of processes like politicisation, mobilisation and assertion involving socially and politically dormant groups.[15] Academic attention has been drawn to the way the social basis of the power structure, especially in village India, has undergone a shift through electoral route (Yadav, 1999, p. 2393).

Focus on states

Sifting through elections related literature in India, one finds greater recognition and acceptance of the emergence of states as analytical units in the last three decades. States are being viewed as having emerged as the platforms where not only the electoral politics but the whole gamut of political and economic processes unfolds, which all have national impact (Kumar, 2017b, p. 277).

Why states have emerged as the preferred analytical units rather than election analysts attempting an 'all-India' based election studies needs to be explained. A foremost factor that has brought focus on the state is the politics of identity taking the centre stage. The upsurge in identity politics has reconfigured the democratic politics of India in the last three decades in a significant way as diverse social groups in India have increasingly been politicised and mobilised on the basis of social cleavages rather than on the basis of their common economic interests or ideology. There have been struggles around the assertiveness and conflicting claims of the identity groups, and of struggles amongst them, often fought out on lines of region, religion, language (even dialect), caste, and community. These struggles have found expressions in the changed mode of electoral representation that has brought the local/regional into focus with the hitherto politically dormant groups and regions finding voices. A more genuinely representative democracy in recent India has led to the sharpening of the line of distinction between or among the identity groups and the regions. These identity groups are sought to be collectively recognised and mobilised either on the basis of caste, tribe, language (script), or dialect. Almost all such social groups are confined spatially to a particular state or sub-region within it, especially after the reorganisation of the states on linguistic/ethnic basis undertaken in the 1950s and 1960s. So invariably, processes of politicisation /mobilisation

/participation take place at the state/state sub-regional level, giving primacy to local/regional over national (Kumar, 2017b).[16]

That this can be an important ground for undertaking political research on Indian states was recognised way back by Weiner (1968), much before the Rath Yatra, Mandal, and the Mandir happened in the 1990s. A pioneer in the discipline, Weiner had argued: 'it (is) at the state level that the conflicts among castes, religious groups, tribes and linguistic groups and factions are played out'. Inevitably, in recent decades, the greater level of recognition of constituent states in the Indian Union as the primary units of analyses has led to the emergence of state politics as an autonomous discipline. Even in the discipline of comparative politics, state-level variances have of late received much more focus in the discussion of themes like ethnic movements, party systems, developmental experiences, political institutions, and democratisation, unlike in the past when India was always referred to in cross-national perspective (Kumar, 2017b).

State level parties

What has also brought focus on the states as critical political spaces is the emergence of the state level parties in the last three decades.[17] The sizable presence of state parties in the successive Lok Sabha and the frequency of coalition governments at the centre after the decline of 'Congress system'[18] has made 'all-India'/ national polity seem little more than the aggregation of the state level politics. The ascendancy of the BJP as the dominant party has not altered the ground situation much. What explains the electoral success of state parties in recent India?

First, it was the advent of the 'post-Congress polity'[19] that ushered in the 'third electoral system'. It was marked by fragmented/regionalised party system which provided the political space to the new political entrepreneurs/ parties.[20]

Second, the incentive to set up state parties for the political entrepreneurs came from coalition/minority governments becoming the norm in the 1990s. Coalition governments were formed as a result of opportunistic alliances, marked by tough bargaining among political parties, either preceding the elections or after, and sometime even much after the government formation. With the strong-centre framework remaining largely intact, alliances pave the way through which the state parties hoped to influence decision-making process at the national level and also to bring resources to their respective states.[21]

Third, in its effort to become a polity-wide party,[22] BJP especially after its 1996 setback[23] entered into state-specific alliances with the state parties like JD (S), BJD, INLD, AGP, TDP, AIADMK, SAD, and Shiv Sena. To begin with it accepted to be junior ally. While these alliances helped the BJP, they also helped the state parties in confronting the weakened Congress and leaders to gain in stature at the national level.[24]

Fourth, the long-term ascendance of the state level/sub-state level parties,[25] coinciding with an endemic decline of the Congress having 'rainbow coalitional social support base'[26] is to a great extent due to ongoing collectivisation[27] and mobilisation veering around social cleavages.[28] These processes have helped in the rise of state/sub-state level parties,[29] a phenomenon now visible even in the 'older' democracies with the long tradition of having only national parties in winning positions.[30]

Until recently, state parties, especially the 'ethnic parties', succeeded more than the 'polity-wide' parties in drawing support from the newly mobilised identity groups. Of late, however, even the BJP has successfully sought the support of the numerically weak marginal groups by holding festivals/resurrecting their community icons like in case of Uttar Pradesh.[31] Following the state parties,[32] it has targeted specially the castes/communities which have remained 'sandwiched' between the upper and middle/intermediate castes and the Scheduled castes. So the polity-wide parties including the Congress are no longer averse to play the identity card with impunity.

Fifth, as the state-based parties openly target and cater to the interests of a particular set of social categories, they show greater potential than the 'polity-wide'[33] parties in being able to activate voter linkages that are sectarian, ethnic, and populist in a clientelistic democracy like India. The state-level parties, particularly if they are 'ethnic parties', gain by openly resorting to identity-based clientelistic politics. National/multi-state parties have to play 'a coded ethnic card, invoking ethnic identities quietly in its selection of candidates but not openly in its identification of issues', seeking the support of ascriptive categories through the 'distribution of patronage but never through the rhetoric of identity' (Chandra, 2004, p. 26).

As a result, the state parties have better potential to create and retain a 'core social constituency' which in turn becomes a distinct 'voting community'.[34] This politics of 'vote bank' more often than not gets them electoral dividend under the single plurality electoral system, especially if there is a multi-polar contest[35] and also that it is a 'normal election' and not a 'wave election', a rarity now.[36]

Sixth, the state parties score over national parties like the Congress[37] and the BJP,[38] whose leadership especially at the higher echelons has remained largely with the elite castes due to lack of adequate institutional mechanism to facilitate the intra-party mobility within their organisations. As a result, leaders having support among under-represented social groups have preferred to form their 'own' parties. That way they hope to exert influence as a coalition ally rather being in a marginal position in the parent party.[39]

Seventh, state parties tend to claim that they can be trusted more than the national parties whenever case of any conflict of inter-state dimension arises, be it over the capital city, highways, airports, trade or over river water/dams.[40] Such claims receive many takers especially as the inter-state competiveness/conflicts have increased.

The emergent phenomenon of the 'federalisation' of party system[41] underlines the need to focus on distinctive character as well as growing autonomy of the state units of the national parties,[42] especially when they have been in the government[43] and in terms of electoral alliances they seek.

Resurgence of state-level leaders

Emergence of states and state-level parties in an increasingly decentred polity, as discussed previously, has led to the resurgence of state leaders, reminiscent of 'Nehru era' satraps in the Congress era. However, unlike them, the new crop of state leaders almost singlehandedly makes crucial policy decisions and their decisions actually affect political happenings in their respective states.[44] As such they leave an indelible imprint over the states' politics. Resurgence of this new crop of state leaders can be attributed to the following factors (Kumar, 2017b, pp. 282–3; Kumar, 2019).

First, with the mode of democracy remaining 'patrimonial' in India, 'patronage' and 'clientelism' catering to primordial identities continue to play a role despite all rhetoric of 'inclusive growth' (Chandra, 2004; Ziegfeld, 2016).[45] State-level leaders in particular playing the role of the 'transactional leaders'[46] directly represent and serve the specific needs, 'not only of territorial constituencies, but frequently the more tangible ones of primordial groups' (Wood, 1984, p. 2) (Burns, 1978). These leaders ensure the direct/visible transfer of public resources to the targeted social constituency in exchange of the electoral support received. Clientelism ensures that the electorates identify themselves with not only the party in power but more so with the party leader as the benefactor/patron.[47] As a result, castes/communities acting as 'political/ voting' categories tend to cling to the leader they consider as their 'own' in a 'realistic' hope of having access to public resources as well as protection, provided the leader comes to power.[48]

Second, given the ascendance of politics of 'presence' and dignity, having their 'men' (hardly any women) in the seat of power also brings 'feel good/ psychic good' factor to the concerned community the leader belongs to, more so if the community in question has been historically on the margin in social and political terms. Even the proven excesses/extravagance of such leaders is condoned/disbelieved by their followers/loyalists.

Third, what explains the power and influence of the state parties' bosses is the sheer size in terms of the territory and population of states that they lord over. Most states are comparable or even bigger than countries in the west. It allows the leaders, especially when they are in power, to gain access to massive 'political resources—organisation, money, votes' besides the bureaucracy if they are in power. This partly explains, more so now than three decades ago as to why 'it is in the states . . . where many of India's most ambitious politicians concentrate their energies', at least in the beginning of their career though they all aim at moving to the centre' (Wood, 1984, p. 2). So, unlike the 'Congress era' when political leaders were able to 'move directly into national politics' after doing stint at the state level, now an increasing number of political leaders have to graduate to 'national' politics only after having had a successful career at the state level. As was then, even now states have been 'training grounds for national politicians' like Narendra Modi (Weiner, 1968, p. 3). With the ascendance of states, however, most of the powerful state-level leaders from the national parties are reluctant to move to the centre as mere union ministers. It was evident in the case of Manohar Parrikar who went back to Goa as chief minister leaving the powerful portfolio of the Defence Minister of India. Shivraj Singh Chauhan, Raman Singh, and Vasundhara Raje, outgoing BJP popular chief ministers have preferred to remain in the state politics.

Fourth, the steady decline in terms of organisational structure and presence[49] and the inability to present ideological alternatives to the electorates afflicting political parties further underlines the criticality of local leadership factor. This is especially true for 'new' parties whose founder-presidents and their 'natural heirs' cultivate their personal community-based support.[50] Depending more on their personal charisma and sphere of influence than deliberately weakened party machinery, these resourceful leaders make and unmake the parties on their own terms. As such, they are instrumental in shaping the form and content of 'their' parties' agenda/manifesto, tenor of election campaigns and also deciding about the important matter of alliance-building. In a democracy like India where 'mass politics' trumps the 'elite politics', it is through the leader and his public speeches during the campaign rather than reading the manifestos or following the party's action that electorates come to know about the party's ideological position on the issues and the reasons behind making or breaking the alliances. Also, given the electoral volatility which is due to weak loyalties/identification of a sizable number of voters to a particular party, the leader plays a crucial role not only to ensure the turnout of the staunch supporters of his party to vote but also swing these floating/indecisive voters' vote. Since Indian states witness high turnout elections, 'lower probability voters (who tend to be younger, poorer, and less educated) make up a larger share of electorate' rather than pro-statuesque core voters having traditional loyalty to a party (Vaishnav and Guy, 2018, p. 73). For these voters the leadership factor plays an important role. This, however, depends as there are many examples when a 'popular' leader has left the parent established party and formed his (all male) 'own' party in the fervent hope of all this but has failed miserably in swinging the vote. Then for these 'transactional leaders', it becomes impossible for them to singlehandedly build the party structure/lower level leadership and keep the loyalists having multiple and competing interests. Yeddiyurappa, Keshubhai Patel, both powerful ethnic leaders belonging to dominant castes from Karnataka and Gujarat, respectively, are some recent examples.

Fifth, thinking in economic terms, the introduction of neo-liberal market-oriented economic policies presented an opportunity to dynamic state leaders like Chandrababu Naidu, Chimanbhai Patel, S. M. Krishna, Narendra

Modi, among others, to take early advantage of the new economic climate to think of the innovative ways to induce growth in the states under their command, instead of looking towards the centre for the policy directions as well as all the funds like in the old 'socialist' days. Significantly, it was in the 1990s that the states under such dynamic leadership grew much faster than others, drawing attention to the leadership impact at the state level in the economic domain. An ambitious and theatrical leader like Modi could deftly use 'Gujarat model' of growth to emerge as a national leader without ever having been situated in the capital in his entire political life.

Sixth, many present-era state leaders have also managed to remain nationally visible not because they are 'national' in their orientation or due to all-India presence of their party, or because their parties are in coalitional government at the centre but also because of the positions they take and issues they articulate and champion, which receive traction in different socio-economic and political contexts other than the state to which they belong.[51]

State leadership: then and now[52]

While focusing on the state leaders, one comes across distinctive forms of political leadership over the period. As mentioned at the outset, there was never a dearth of state leaders in India having their distinctive leadership styles. There was, of course, an interim period defined by person-centred centralising leadership of Indira Gandhi when state leadership was not allowed to flourish. In this interim period state leaders were shuffled at will and were expected to remain low-profile/self-effacing[53] for their survival so that they did not appear like a threat to the Congress 'high command' (read the Nehru-Gandhi family). Those who appeared gaining or becoming ambitious politically like Kamalapati Tripathi, Hemwati Nandan Bahuguna, among others, were swiftly purged. Dissenters like Devraj Urs had to leave the party though they remained important leaders. Even then, with the threat of president rule hanging on their head, non-Congress parties did have a string of state leaders who could deal with the central state and were difficult to be dislodged like Jyoti Basu, Ramakrishna Hegde, N. T. Rama Rao, as well as Dravidian leaders like Karunanidhi and M.G. Ramachandran.[54]

How does one compare the emergent state leaders in 'new' India, mostly belonging to the state-level parties and drawing support from the middle/lower castes with the 'old' generation of state-level party bosses and 'machine-men' like the ones within the Congress, often referred as 'regional satraps' in Nehruvian 'socialist' India? Has not the old 'Congress era' politics of patronage continued unabated in the form of distribution of goods, services, funds, loans, government contracts through networks of clients to the targeted social constituency by the leader in the fervent hope of winning the electoral support (Kumar, 2019c)?

Drawing from the classical literature on political leadership in Indian context may be helpful in reflecting about the two different generations of leaders operating in two different social-economic environments. Referring to the first generation of leaders, Morris-Jones had referred to three different 'languages' of Indian politics namely modern, traditional, and saintly. His formulation was inspired by Weberian 'pure types' of political leadership in the forms of 'traditional/patriarchal'; the charismatic/confrontational; and the 'bureaucratic/rationality ordered' (Weber, 1978).[55] In his definition of 'language', Morris-Jones included the 'manners, styles, idioms and fashions' in which 'political life' is conducted in modern India. He argued that the 'contrast between modern and traditional languages is a contrast between the political institutions (system) of a nation-state and the (social) structure of an ancient society which far from having grown up together, have only just been introduced to each other' (Morris-Jones, 1964, p. 52).[56] He observed that political leaders were 'bilingual' in the sense that as law-makers and ministers they used modern constitutional language based on democratic values but while interacting with their rustic followers/unwashed masses, they still had to resort to the traditional language of caste, community, and customs in order to connect. These leaders in order to be electable were to transcend both modern (public) as well as traditional (private) domains that divided the political landscape of the then India. Arguably, it was more correct for the 'minor'/'micro-political' leaders like legislators/constituency/panchayat-level leaders but not the state-level top leaders who could be counted like the national level 'macro-political leaders' (Forrester, 1966, 312). Congress bosses who wielded power and influence over a long term, like Chandrabhanu Gupta, K. Kamraj, Bidhan Chandra Roy, Pratap Singh Kairon, Yashwant Singh Parmar, Sri Krishna Sinha, Mohanlal Sukharia, Neelam Sanjeeva Reddy, S. Nijalingappa, D.P. Mishra, and Ravi Shanker Shukla, among others, they all carried a nationalist perspective and agenda and hardly saw themselves as regional/state-level leaders (Kumar, 2017b).[57] Mostly of middle-class origin, well-educated, and having led the Congress-led nationalist movement in their respective states in their youth, their political visions and practices were modern and national. At the same time these 'liberal, sophisticated' leaders were also 'men of the people' making 'earnest efforts to identify themselves with village India and communicate in a traditional language' as now in an electoral democracy their spheres of operation were limited to the states and they had to 'communicate to electorates living in village India' (Forrester, 1966, p. 312). At the same time the internal democracy and a dialogic culture within the party organisation allowed them to feel being part of the national mainstream and have national impact also especially in the times of crisis within the party, like over succession issue after death of Nehru or Shastri.

One could even say the same about non-Congress political leaders like E.M.S. Namboodiripad or even Jyoti Basu, both essentially state-level leaders with a national presence due to their influence over the Communist Party which despite its limited electoral success was viewed as the ideological alternative of the centrist Congress.[58] Chaudhary Charan Singh, essentially a Kisan leader from Uttar Pradesh, succeeded in gaining some national stature after becoming Prime Minister at a time when newly economically empowered peasant castes were feeling restless for being denied share in political and economic terms under the Congress regime. Sheikh Abdullah and C. Annadurai, leading two of the oldest cadre-based and ideologically oriented state parties[59] i.e. NC (1939) and DMK (1949), respectively, could be considered notable exceptions to the older genre, though they also 'eventually abandoned secessionism for a place within the Indian Constitution' (Guha, 2010, p. 290).

Besides having bilingual leaders,[60] the bygone era had another similarity. Politics then was imagined at the national level, even among the local electorates. It was evident in the fact that it was possible for leaders from one state to contest elections in neighbouring states[61] and also move on to the national politics. The robust internal organisational structure and dialogic culture within the parties allowed politically grounded state-based leaders to influence party decisions even at the national level. All this changed with decimation of the party organisation and institutionalised leadership structure during Indira Gandhi regime, followed not surprisingly by other parties as well. Many of these 'new' parties were formed by leaders defecting from the Congress after the failed experiment of Janata Party. These newly formed regional/state parties tracing their lineage from the Congress and Socialist Parties prospered in the post-Mandal India. The founder presidents of these parties, mostly still alive,[62] have been primarily concerned with consolidating their personal support base within their respective states and also ensuring that their families control the parties after they are gone. These ambitious leaders have had their opportunity before the rise of the BJP to share real power at the centre and as in the case of Lalu Yadav act even as 'king makers'. What also helped these parties was the fact that, under the emergent fragmented electoral system, the electorates were no longer diffident to vote for them as was the case in the Congress era when there used to be a question mark over their winnability potential and also the threat that the candidate they help to win would not be able to be part of the government and thus unable to dole out largesse.

With the boundaries between state-level parties and the state units of national parties becoming blurred in terms of their support base or agenda, and vulnerability of the Congress and even the ascendant BJP to win Lok Sabha elections on their own, powerful state leaders like Mamata Banerjee, Mulayam Singh Yadav or Mayawati and Lalu Yadav and Nitish Kumar not long ago, have for long nurtured national ambitions which are reflected in their concerted effort to come together against the BJP and a much weakened Congress as 2019 elections approach. However, what remains a handicap for these leaders is their lack of nation-wide stature, given their susceptibility to fall prey to regional and parochial interests to the detriment of the national cause on evidence when they have held posts in the government at the centre.

Worse, almost every state party leader has already or is in the process of transforming 'his/her' party into a family/dynastic party, even the ones like Sharad Pawar or P. A. Sangma who left the Congress on this very ground. For this purpose these dynasts keep the party organisation deliberately weak from the beginning and also control the party funds (Chhibber, 2013; Diwakar, 2017, p. 145). Dynastic mode of politics relates to the large returns associated with these state offices and the leader wants to hand over the gains to his/her progenies (Chandra, 2016). These leaders' concerns and awareness about societal issues remain restricted to the family, communities/regions they primarily rely on for electoral support, or the state they belong to. They know little or next to nothing of the problems of anything as big as India nor do they make an attempt to know.[63] Even within the state, it is a particular caste or a cluster of castes or communities that form the core of these community leaders' politics, though they all spout the secular language of development and governance. 'Saintly' idioms of sacrifice and austerity which Morris-Jones referred in the context of Nehruvian India are long forgotten and not even valued. Hardly any of the newly emergent leaders can qualify as a 'transformational' leader having long-term vision. This is true not only for the state parties' leaders but also the state-based leaders belonging to the national parties even though some of them are made party in-charge of other states also. In contrast, the old generation leaders, steeped in the nationalist tradition and avowing the agenda of 'nation-building', did not see themselves primarily as caste/community leaders and also their politics and policies were not governed so starkly by narrow considerations of caste, community, and region. With a sense of prescience, as early as in the 1960s, Sirsikar had predicted that as 'a consequence of the strength of regionalism', political leadership 'based on tradition of sacrifice, dedication and austerity' would be replaced by 'new' leaders who would 'represent their hold on their regions, either due to caste or interest group support' (1965, p. 522).

The 'new' leaders are, however, comparable to the 'old' party bosses of the Congress in the sense that both genres of leaders continue to belong to/have the support of the numerically significant elite/dominant castes of their respective states. The difference lies in terms of the hierarchical positioning as earlier, the leaders would always be from upper/elite castes, whereas now middle and upper-backward numerically strong peasant castes, beneficiary of land reforms/Green Revolution, public education system in Indian languages and governmental affirmative action have also joined in having powerful leaders (Jaffrelot, 2015). However, in the case of national parties like Congress, BJP, and the CPI (M), even now the state leadership remains largely with the upper/dominant castes largely due to the lack of adequate institutional mechanisms to facilitate the intra-party mobility within the party organisations. In the coming decades, however, even these parties would be forced to bring in more leaders from non-elite castes, given the nature of representational politics that has evolved. Realising the need to broaden its social support base, BJP has consciously drafted in leaders from the backward castes with mixed results. Among the early appointments were Kalyan Singh and Uma Bharati as chief ministers from Uttar Pradesh and Madhya Pradesh, respectively. In more recent times, Shivraj Singh Chauhan, the outgoing three-term former chief minister from MP is the only prominent face from the OBC category in the party.

There is an important aspect in which the present generation of state leaders score over the political leaders of yesteryears and that is their apparently greater tenacity and ability to manoeuvre in much more uncertain political waters. The regional satraps within the Congress, howsoever influential they might have been, moved within the party hierarchy steadily, adhering to the party's culture and ideology and led with the help of established institutions and committed party workers. Apart of their individual skill, they benefitted from being in an established party with a secure support base and resources along with a vast amount of goodwill due to party's role in the nationalist struggle. Almost all of them started as followers and confirmed diligently to the established rules of political game.

State parties' leaders of today have to set their own rules of game. They almost singlehandedly shape the culture, organisation, and agenda of the parties they form and lead from the front. This in fact has become true even in the case of older state parties like SAD or DMK, which no longer remain the cadre-based movement parties of yore. In fact for long these parties have been under the firm control of their long-serving leaders Parkash Singh Badal and Karunanidhi, shedding their organisational advantage and yet doing well electorally.

There is another respect in which the new generation of risk-taking state leaders distinguish themselves. Since most of these 'new' state leaders have invariably left their parent parties to form a new party with an uncertain electoral future, they need to nurture a much greater degree of empathy/bonding/accessibility/communication with their followers to galvanise the party workers. Even having a famous family name or access to family wealth does not guarantee instant success to a succeeding political leader as has been evident in the case of Y.S. Jaganmohan Reddy. Moreover, as 'transactional' leaders pitted against the well-established and often more senior leaders of older established parties, they need to promise and actually win elections to be able to provide resources and services to their followers. So in their case, 'agency of the leader' becomes a critical determinant (Wyatt, 2015, p. 175). As 'political entrepreneurs', many of these leaders are able to set the terms of electoral discourse with their innovative ways to capture the peoples imagination like in the case of Arvind Kejriwal,[64] the Aam Aadmi Party (AAP) convener and Delhi Chief Minister, and can even be credited to have 'systemic relevance' in the states they operate and to an extent even at the national level (Wyatt, 2015, p. 167). These skills are much more needed for the state parties to survive particularly as of now given the formidable challenge in form of an ascendant BJP led by a 'maximum leader' like Modi, who was ably assisted by powerful state-level BJP leadership, out to establish its electoral hegemony. Even the Congress in a spot now after repeated electoral setbacks still remains one of the two leading parties in large states like Karnataka, Maharashtra, Rajasthan, Chhattisgarh, and Madhya Pradesh, besides many other states.[65] As an impending challenge, it is much more difficult for the minor parties' leaders like Ramvilas Paswan of LJP or Anupriya Patel of Apna Dal who need to constantly negotiate/forge alliances with the major parties in order to survive electorally and get a place in the coalition government despite being an ally. This is not enough. These 'minor' leaders also need to project themselves as ones offering something 'different': An 'alternative' to the electorates or a tough act to follow. It is the projection of their leadership model and capability that help them to distinguish themselves and their parties, given the fact that there has been a large-scale convergence on major social and economic ideology/policies among parties in recent decades. Besides, building up a party requires the founding leader to invest 'considerable time, energy and money' to keep the party machinery going elections after elections, given the frequency of elections in India (Wyatt, 2010, p. 166).

To sum up, the ongoing political processes of federalisation/regionalisation may have provided impetus to the rise of states, state parties, and state-level leadership, but these related developments have not led to any positive change in the nature of state level politics despite greater mobilisation and participation of marginal social groups. The emergent state parties have mostly degenerated into 'family parties' controlled by dynasts. As these 'new' state-level leaders come from different social background in comparison to their counterparts from the Congress era, they make India's democracy look much more representative. Given their middle/backward castes social background, they to some extent have been instrumental in triggering greater mobilisation and participation of hitherto neglected social groups across the states, championing the politics of presence and dignity. However, in their outlook, actions, and leadership style, they remain overtly narrow focused socially as well as regionally. Being primarily 'transactional leaders' in an electoral democracy and surviving on patronage and clientelism, their main concerns remain to cater to their 'voting community', constituted primarily on the basis of caste/community/region. As result, they often neglect the governance- related aspects of policies and development at a larger scale, which is much needed even for the social constituency they claim to represent.

Notes

1 This makes it methodologically also very useful for longitudinal analysis of India's electoral politics.
2 India as an electoral democracy stands out for three factors. First, poor and illiterate tend to vote in larger percentages than the educated and rich electorates. Second, unlike the 'old' democracies of the west, in India electoral participation and contestation as well as the number of parties that have witnessed a rise in

recent decades. Third, the electoral participation in India goes up in the elections held for lower bodies unlike the western democracies where voter turnout is higher for higher bodies' elections.

3 India's 17th Lok Sabha election with around 930 million voters was not only the biggest election in the world history but possibly also the biggest ever human-managed event, political or sports.

4 Considering the number of parties in the fray sometime it seems leaders even tend to outnumber their followers! Rise of the BJP as a colossal party, however, is ominous news for the small/minor parties as impending defections loom large over them.

5 Sheikh Abdullah (NC), E. M. S. Namboodiripad (CPI), respectively from Jammu and Kashmir and Kerala enjoyed national level stature despite being confined to their respective states.

6 'The coexistence of trust and a celebratory endorsement as well as a critical assessment makes India's electoral politics a meaningful activity deserving serious scholarly attention and decoding' (Palshikar, 2013, p. 164).

7 'Since her independence in 1947, parliamentary democracy has been the central mechanism governing India. . . . In a sense; elections form the essence of Indian democracy' (Kondo, 2007, p. 2).

8 Das (2009, p. 90) refers to the institution of elections as the 'lifeblood of democracy' in India.

9 Local bodies' elections, like Assembly elections, register greater electoral participation. Also, individual candidates/local leaders play greater role in influencing the verdict compared to Lok Sabha elections.

10 Palshikar (2013, p. 164) argues that elections in India not only lead to popular mobilisation but also facilitate the 'elite control' by ordinary citizens, bereft of 'material or symbolic resources'.

11 Palshikar (2013, p. 163) underlines the need to make a distinction between 'writings on elections' and 'election studies'.

12 Institutional-legal components of electoral democracy like the role of the election commission, electoral rules, electoral finance, electoral reformist law, and judicial discourses have received academic attention, though focus has been more on the electoral/political processes (Macmillan, 2010; Sridharan and Vaishnav, 2016; Sondhi, 2016, pp. 196–212).

13 'The period since 1977 has been marked by many substantial changes, in the nature of electoral politics and the structure of party competition, at both all-India level and in most states of Indian Union . . . the party system and electoral competition finally appeared to be changing and making way for a new structure of competition' (Palshikar, 2013, p. 161).

14 For an overview of the election studies that concern recent India, reference may be made of Kondo (2007), Lama-Rewal (2009), and Palshikar (2013).

15 As a result, legislative bodies have become more representative as middle and backward castes are elected in greater numbers. Still the representation of minorities and especially women has been much less than their demographic proportion. TMC and BJD leadership gave one third of party tickets to women candidates in 2019 elections.

16 In the post-poll surveys across the country conducted by Lokniti-Centre for the Study of Developing Societies (CSDS), Delhi in 1996 and 1999 Lok Sabha elections, 53 and 51 percent of the respondents respectively prioritised region/state they belonged to over the country while deciding about their electoral choices.

17 State parties had won at least 40 percent of the vote polled in the parliamentary elections in the 1990s and until 2014, more than any other country in the world (Ziegfeld, 2016, p. 3).
    eci.nic.in/eci_main/archiveofge2014/20%20-20Performance%20of%20 National%20Parties.pdf

18 Rajni Kothari (1964) described the party system of India until the 1967 elections as the 'Congress system'. He referred to the organisational ability of the Congress to create a wider social coalitional support base, enabling the party to win elections both at the state as well federal level. Congress acted also as a hegemonic party representing the ideological consensus. 'One-party dominant system' was understood as the very essence of the political system of early independent India (Brass, 1965; Weiner, 1967; Sission, 1972).

19 Yadav referred to Assembly elections verdicts in 16 states of India in the early 1990s as the beginning of a 'competitive multi-party system, which no longer is defined with reference to the Congress' (1996, p. 95). As a consequence, Congress learnt to 'transform itself from the dominant party in a dominant party system to a competitive party in a multi-party system' (Rudolph and Rudolph, 2008, p. 36).

20 The last three decades have witnessed 'the consolidation of the non-Congress space as well as the decline of the Congress and, in some cases, fragmentation of the state level party system' (Sridharan, 2014, p. 23).

21 Dravidian parties when in coalition government at the centre have insisted on getting the key ministries like telecom, commerce, and industries.

22 While a polity-wide party contests and wins across the country, a state party is basically confined to a particular state. Uniquely, a polity-wide party in India contests also at the local level.

23 BJP, despite forming the government in 1996 by virtue of being the largest party in the Lok Sabha, could not remain in office due to its inability to get the support of the state parties.

24 Appreciative of this fact, BJP has continued with its alliance even with the difficult allies like Shiv Sena and JD (U).

25 Sridharan (2012, p. 326) puts 'regional parties with a single-state stronghold' into three major categories: Hindu nationalist (the Shiv Sena); agrarian/lower-caste populist (the Janata Party and its offshoots like SP, RJD, RLD, BJD, JD (S), JD (U); ethnic/ ethno-regional parties based on particular regional linguistic groups (DMK, AIADMK, SAD, TDP, AGP) or lower-caste blocs (BSP) or tribes (JMM). Ziegfeld (2012, pp. 72–3) defines a party as a regional party if it 'draws electoral support from a narrow geographical base'. A regional party differs from a regionalist party as the latter 'openly appeals to a region (or regions) to the exclusion of others and makes that central to its strategy of mobilising voters'.

    Ayyangar and Jacob (2014, p. 235) have divided state-based parties into ethnic, territorial, and ad hoc splinter parties: 'ethnic parties are primarily interested in the mobilisation and empowerment of particular ethnic groups . . . and aim to capture state power to redistribute resources to their targeted groups. Territorial parties mobilise citizens within their respective states. . . . Their focus is geographical, and they are concerned with issues such as self-determination, regional autonomy or simply access to a larger share of national resources. Adhoc splinter parties are usually too small to aspire to come to power by themselves even at the state level'.

26 Attributing the decline of the Congress party as an umbrella party to 'the desertion of the party by social groups that once supported it in a number of states', Farooqui and Sridharan (2016, p. 331) have raised question as to 'whether a Congress-type, encompassing, umbrella party can survive the sharpened politicisation of social cleavages, in the Indian case, religious, caste and regional cleavages since such a party will tend to lose out to parties based on religious, caste and regional identities in identitarian outbidding'.

27 Different castes and sub-castes OBCs have come together for political gains. Gope, Gwala, Ahir-all these castes are now being identified and mobilised as Yadav caste in Hindi speaking states. Similarly of late there has been an attempt to bring Patidar/Patel and Kunbi communities in Gujarat nearer to Kurmi community in north Indian Hindi-speaking states of Bihar and Uttar Pradesh.

28 In the 2015 Assembly elections in Bihar, the 'local' appeared more significant than the 'national' as was reflected in the slogan 'Bihari' versus 'Bahri'. Also in the 2017 Punjab Assembly elections, AAP lost out as local Punjabi leadership was subordinated to outsiders like Sanjay Singh and Durgesh Pathak. Modi using his Gujarati origin was successful in turning verdict in favour of Gujarat assembly election.

29 Himachal Pradesh and Uttarakhand are two notable exceptions. The two north Indian states stand out for having significant percentage of upper castes (twice-born) people who have shown inclination to vote for the national parties, as revealed in the CSDS-Lokniti surveys.

30 In Great Britain, regional parties have emerged strongly in Scotland, Northern Ireland, and Wales as a large segment of the electorates in these regions are no longer convinced about the ability of the national parties to protect and support their regional interests and demands. Same is the case with the French-speaking Quebec region in Canada.

31 One can refer to caste support-based state parties like RJD, JD (U),SP, INLD, to name only a few. Then, there are state parties which primarily mobilise support based on sub-regional territorialised identity like the TDP, AGP, TRS, YSR Congress and PDP, among others.

32 JD (U) in Bihar and SP in Uttar Pradesh have mobilised the lower OBCs and lower Scheduled castes by treating them as distinct social categories for service delivery.

33 Usage of the term seems somewhat problematic in the case of India as neither of the two 'polity-wide' parties can claim to have spread uniformly or have been in a winning position across the states (Kailash, 2014a).

34 AIUDF, the Assam-based party established in 2005, managed to emerge as main opposition party of Assam, winning 18 out of 126 seats in the Assembly elections held in 2011. Despite setback in 2016 elections, the party banking on 34.2 percent of the Muslim population in Assam, which constitute the majority in 9 out of 29 districts territorially concentrated in Lower Assam/ Barak Valley regions, remains electorally relevant.

35 BSP and SP were able to form majority governments by receiving respectively 30 and 29 percent of the votes polled respectively in 2007 and 2012 Assembly elections in Uttar Pradesh.

36 Ziegfeld (2012) argues that the electorates in a 'clientelistic democracy' like India vote for a party with the aims as divergent as to extract the material benefits and becoming beneficiaries of direct transfer of state resources and services, or simply because their votes are bought.

37 Weiner (1967) has pointed out that the Congress leaders promoted lower castes political leaders primarily to strengthen their position in the factional fights within the organisation.

38 Realising the electoral need, BJP has consciously drafted in leaders from the backward castes in post-Mandal era with mixed results.

39 Despite Supreme Court putting a blanket ban on the electoral use of caste, community and religion, and the sectarian appeal to the voters, it was very much visible during the election campaign in 2019. ECI lacking sufficient punitive powers could only ban the defaulters from campaigning for two to three days.

40 SAD-BJP coalition government got the legislative bill passed in March 2016 to de-notify the acquired land for the purpose of building Sutlej-Yamuna link canal that would have enabled Haryana to receive river water from Punjab.

41 Yadav and Palshikar (2009b, p. 55) argue that electoral choices even for the Lok Sabha elections are increasingly being 'derived' from 'competitive format, electoral cycle, political agenda, participatory pattern and social cleavages defined in state politics'.

42 There is a distinction between state party and regional party. CPI and CPM, for instance, may not be dubbed as 'regional' parties and much less 'national/polity-wide' parties if we consider that their support base is confined to Kerala, West Bengal, and Tripura, which fall in three different geographical regions of India (Sridharan, 2012, p. 339).

43 The economic policies of the CPM led left front governments formed in the last decade in Kerala and West Bengal led by V.S. Achuthanandan and Buddhadeb Bhattacharjee, respectively, differed starkly. One can also refer to the divergence of positions in the Congress state units of Congress in neighbouring Punjab and Haryana. Party leaders of the two states never campaign in each other's state whereas leaders of INLD and SAD do campaign for each other.

44 One can refer to the decision by Chandrababu Naidu to build a new capital city Amravati for truncated Andhra Pradesh at a huge cost to the state exchequer.

45 'Clientelism is a term which describes the distribution of selective benefits to individuals or clearly defined groups in exchange for political support' (Hopkin, 2009, p. 406).

46 A 'transactional' leader has a give and take/contractual relationship with his/her supporters. However, over the years it also develops into an emotional bond especially as the leader is witnessed as 'provider' for electorates. Jaya Lalitha and YS Rajasekhara Reddy were such leaders (Kumar, 2019).

47 It is very common in India to find the picture of chief ministers on the ambulance, public distribution cards, or even on the flood relief materials. State governments if from the opposition invariably pass on central government-funded schemes as their own.

48 The electoral choices, however, may shift drastically in case of 'non-performance' by the leader and also in case of 'exceptional/wave' elections.

49 Even the much older, cadre-based and ideologically rooted parties like SAD, DMK, and NC have fallen victims to 'dynastic politics'. These parties are also becoming populist and catch-all electoralist parties, shedding their ideological moorings.

50 Reference here can be made of leaders like Lalu Yadav, Bal Thackeray, Sharad Pawar, Ram Vilas Paswan, Ajit Singh, Udhav Thakre, among many others. The 'inheritors', of course, need to renew their electoral legitimacy showing their leadership skill and performance like in successful case of Naveen Patnaik, Udhav Thackeray, and Jagan Mohan Reddy.

51 Arvind Kejriwal on his debut as a politician succeeded in drawing the nationwide attention by prioritising the issue of corruption in the run-up to 2014 elections.

52 Kumar (2019, pp. 277–8).

53 James Manor has referred to the political style of Digvijay Singh, two-term Congress chief minister of undivided Madhya Pradesh, which was marked by a degree of reticence/self-effacement. It was in contrast to 'person-centred' high profile of another developmental leader Chandrababu Naidu, then chief minister of undivided Andhra Pradesh (Manor, 2010, p. 197).

54 Even within the Congress, powerful state-level leaders like Devraj Urs took cudgels with Indira Gandhi, though they were few.

55 Weber believed that these three forms of leader/follower relations occur in combination and 'there may be gradual transitions between these types'.

56 He argues that traditional India contained a different kind of politics from that of the 'modern' state (Morris-Jones, p. 52).

57 Kamraj Plan, ostensibly implemented to allow the Congress leaders to devote themselves full time to party's organisational work after leaving the government, was also viewed as a veiled attempt by powerful 'syndicate' to purge 'inconvenient' national leaders like Morarji Desai. The same syndicate, comprising of the regional satraps, played an important role in party's choice of two Prime Ministers after Nehru.

58 Jyoti Basu was denied primeministership by his own party polit bureau under a coalitional arrangement agreed upon by non-Congress and non-BJP parties.
59 Like the DMK and NC, SAD has had its ideological roots autonomous of the Congress party.
60 Dravidian parties' leaders have traditionally used a distinct 'ornamental and alliterative' variant of Tamil in their public speaking that can be attributed to their background in cinema. The same theatrical mode of politics interspersed with flowery Tamil is likely to continue as two new entrants to Tamil politics post-Jaya Lalitha; i.e. Rajnikanth and Kamal Hassan are cine superstars (Wyatt, 2010).
61 Madhya Pradesh for a long time had a particularly strong tradition of 'outsider politicians' from Uttar Pradesh and Maharashtra.
62 Indian political leaders usually have a much longer life than an average Indian and also with very few exceptions they hardly die when in power! Having access to the best of medical facilities provided at the cost of public exchequer may be a factor but this also testifies to the fact that only the most resilient ones can survive and succeed in the volatile world of Indian politics.
63 State parties' leaders, when in the government under a coalitional arrangement, tend to go all out to benefit their own states and also spend most of their time politicking at the state level.
64 Kejriwal and Modi both run person-centred campaigns, which is reminiscent of Indira Gandhi who used to bypass the party machinery to have direct connect with the electorates.
65 The short-term decision of BSP and SP to set aside a three-decade-old animosity between their leadership and jointly take on BJP in the 2019 Lok Sabha elections can be taken as an example.

2 Punjab politics in comparative perspective

As discussed in the preceding chapter, there has been much recognition and appreciation of states being viewed as important units for developing a theoretical framework for analysing politics including electoral politics. The ongoing regionalisation of the polity and economy has led to the emergence of states, both as prime actors as well as arenas where politics takes shape on the ground and has wider impact. Arguably, because of the ongoing de-cantering of India's polity and economy, each state is becoming like a 'mini democracy'. Individual states are now being considered critical to a nuanced understanding of issues in emergent national politics, be it the study of party systems, elections or electoral behaviour.

The fact that the advantage of the comparative method has not been adequately explored may be attributed to the presence of several patterns of state politics as well as extreme fluidity in the nature of state electoral politics. The argument goes that 'all of the Indian states are special cases, each possessing particular historical, geographical, cultural, or economic conditions'. However, a careful study of the emerging trends in Indian politics does reveal certain commonalities across the constituent states in Indian Union who have uniform institutions and laws (Kumar, 2009). This applies to the electoral politics also (Kumar, 2003).

While contextualising Punjab, it does not seem to be an exception to the overall state-level electoral trends, visible across India in recent decades.

First, like in case of other states of India,[1] three historically, socially, and culturally constituted regions namely Malwa, Doaba, and Majha have emerged in the state as electoral regions[2] having their own electoral specificities in terms of issues and choices.[3]

Second, there has been a legacy of politicisation of social cleavages. Caste, kinship, region, language and religion have always remained latent factors, shaping the dynamics of party competition in Punjab as would be discussed in the following sections. Unlike the other states, religion and language have played much more important role in post-partition period. Both factors were behind Punjabi Suba movement in the 1950s and 1960s, followed by dharam yudh morcha ('righteous war') that started in August 1982 from the premises of the golden temple (Darbar Sahib), Sikh identity–based demands have been at the core of Anandpur Sahib Resolutions passed by the Akali Dal in 1973.[4]

Third, since the cessation of militancy, the state has been witness to emergence of stable bipolarity like most of the states in India (with few notable exceptions like Bihar and Uttar Pradesh). Since 1997, political power has alternated between the Congress and the SAD-BJP combine. Even before, there were attempts to secure electoral alliances especially after reorganisation of the state in 1966 (refer the alliance between the Bharatiya Jan Sangh and the Akali Dal or Akali Dal-Janata Party alliance in the 1970s). It was only in 2017 that AAP emerging as the main opposition party raised some hope of the possibility of three-party system.

Fourth, the state has long been witness to 'regular oscillation' in the form of ruling party being voted out in each election and being replaced by the leading opposition party, much before anti-incumbency became a norm than an aberration in state politics in India in the 1980s and 1990s.[5] At the time of this writing, the 2012 election was the sole exception to this trend when the SAD-BJP combine was able to retain power in the state (Kumar, 2012a).[6]

Fifth, the state has been witness to what can be termed as unveiling of a process of 'federalisation of party system' in the sense that the SAD, a state level party, has been the dominant partner in a coalitional arrangement with the BJP being a junior partner. State unit of the Congress, a national party, has equally been keen to raise the state specific issues. In 2004, it was the Congress government led by Captain Amarinder Singh, which was instrumental in getting the 'Punjab Termination of Agreement Act, 2004' by the state legislative assembly, having the wrath of the party high command.

Sixth, with 'patrimonial' mode of democratic politics on the ascent especially in the states having the presence of 'ethnic' parties,[7] Punjab has also been witness to the rise of competitive populism as the contending parties (Congress being very much part) in a closely contested electoral arena have routinely indulged in patronage, clientelism, and hollow promises for securing votes.

Punjab 'exceptionalism'

A recurrent theme interweaving most of the studies of state politics in recent India is the phenomenon designated as 'democratic upsurge'.[8] Most north Indian states following on the footsteps of the states of south India are viewed as experimenting with what has been dubbed as a 'silent revolution' with political power 'being transferred, on the whole peacefully, from the upper-caste elites to various subaltern groups. . . . The relative calm . . . is primarily due to the fact that the whole process is incremental' (Jaffrelot, 2003, p. 494). Factors such as challenge to the legitimacy of traditional social authority in ritualistic sense, relative economic empowerment due to forces of modernisation, public policies of affirmative action, and also the changed nature of electoral participation and representation are viewed as paving the way for the assertion and subsequent empowerment of the hitherto politically dormant socially marginal groups across the Indian states.[9]

In terms of 'presence', a new generation of political entrepreneurs and parties representing the socially marginal communities has come up in recent decades. This 'quiet transfer' of political power in most states has mainly taken place through an 'electoral route' except for the ones like Kerala and Tamil Nadu, which have also experienced radical reformist movement politics, led by the well-organised parties having pro-lower-caste support base.

The politics of Punjab, however, deviates from the emergent trend. The social basis of power in Punjab has remained unchanged in favour of the land-owning Jat Sikh community despite the sizable presence of the Scheduled castes and the backward castes in the state (Judge, 2012, p. 18).[10] Punjab is yet to experience what has been dubbed as 'assertion from below',[11] sweeping Indian states through electoral route. The near absence of the marginal castes, especially Scheduled castes, in positions of political power in the state even after more than seven decades of political democracy can be attributed to the following three factors.

First, one can refer to the enduring nature of skewed land relations in the state which goes back to colonial era. In a largely peasant state where ownership of land has always been the marker of social and political power status, Scheduled castes suffer with the dubious distinction of possessing lowest share in the agricultural land in the state in the country (2.34 percent). Scheduled castes cultivate only 0.4 percent of all landholdings and own merely 0.72 percent of the cultivable land in the state. This is despite them constituting one third of population in the state (Ram, 2004, p. 898).[12] What further compounds the problem of the landlessness is the unwillingness of the dominant castes especially among the Jat Sikhs to sell their land to the Scheduled castes, defying market logic (Ram, 2012, p. 642). In historical terms, the landlessness among the Scheduled castes can be traced to passage of the Alienation of Land Act way back in 1901 by the colonial regime. The Act provided uniqueness to the social-political structure in an undivided Punjab creating/reinforcing the rural-urban divide by linking the Act to religious- and caste-based identities. The Act further strengthened the traditional structure of deprivation and discrimination in rural Punjab. Under the Act, only the feudal 'agriculturalist' castes/communities' dubbed as 'martial race'-the Sikhs (and the Muslims) were entitled for the allotment of the land in the newly constructed canal colonies of north-west Punjab as the British deliberately made effort to recreate within them 'the rural structure of the rest of the Punjab with all its social and political control' (Talbot, 1980, p. 83). Castes not designated as 'agriculturalist' were barred from acquiring the agricultural land anywhere in Punjab. This deprived the socially marginal castes despite their being dependent over agriculture. Colonial policy was apparently aimed at winning abiding loyalty of the politically quiescent but socially and economically dominant land owning peasant castes and communities that formed significant part of the colonial forces (Stern, 2001, p. 50).[13] Despite the attempted land reforms measures undertaken after independence, the land holding pattern in the state has not undergone any significant change in favour of the marginal castes. More than 60 percent of landed property in rural Punjab remains under the ownership of the Jat Sikh community who constitute around 20 percent of the state population. In more recent times, the success of Green Revolution further accentuated the class divide in rural Punjab as landless/farming labour Scheduled castes community in the state were reduced to the deplorable status of seasonal labourers due to the mechanisation of capital-intensive agriculture. Benefits of the Green Revolution with its 'betting on the strong' strategy mostly went to the rich farmers, as they became recipients of the huge state subsidies in the name of increasing productivity of food-grains. The pattern of land holdings also underwent change in the form of consolidation of landed properties under the Pratap Singh Kairon led Congress regime. It meant that the small farmers, mostly from lower castes, either ceased to remain tenants or were compelled to sell out their land to the big landlords. Incidents of atrocities committed on the Scheduled castes in the absence of any strict implementation of the protective legislation, failure to fulfil the demand of redistribution of the village common land property ('shamlat') among the Scheduled castes,[14] continuing decline in real wages of agricultural labourers in the face of oversupply of rural labour from poorer states of India like Bihar and Uttar Pradesh and no great increase of industrial employment in urban areas—all have gradually alienated the Scheduled castes from the mainstream parties (Mendelssohn and Vicziany, 2000, pp. 170–5).

Second, social cleavages come in the way of their collective mobilisation of the Scheduled castes for electoral purposes. They reflect also on the electoral choices of the communities, precluding the possibility of emergence of an effective party/leadership having a lower-caste base (Judge, 2012, p. 18). Besides being divided on the basis of caste, varying religious allegiance within the Scheduled castes community as they adhere to Christianity, Sikhism, Buddhism, Hinduism, as well as varying sects/Deras comes in the way of mobilisation of the Scheduled castes community as a 'political community'. What also divides these different Scheduled castes is intense competition for the limited benefits of direct patronage that the party in power offers in a sectarian manner (Kumar, 2004).

Third, what allowed the SAD to mask the inner fault-lines on caste lines within the Sikh community with some success by invoking the narratives of Sikh struggles and sacrifices in the past as well as use of religious symbols due to the movements launched in the name of panth, i.e. Punjabi Suba movement and Dharam Yudh Morchas, followed by the rise in militancy in the 1980s.[15] However, even during the height of religious nationalism, Sikh lower-castes were not completely swayed by SAD. Lack of lower caste support, especially among Mazhabi electorates, constituting the majority of landless farming labourers, was due to the fact that the party continued to be viewed as the party of land-owning exploitative Jat Sikhs (Kinnvall, 2006, p. 99). As for the BSP, a Scheduled castes support–based 'ethnic party' founded in 1984 did have an impressive debut in the state politics with its founder Kanshi Ram, a Punjabi from Doaba region, winning the unreserved seat of Hoshiarpur (now reserved) in the 1991 parliamentary elections. BSP went on to win nine constituencies in the 1992 Assembly elections with 16.32 percent of the vote share, contesting from 105 seats. Since then, however, it has been a story of constant decline for the party. The sizable demographic presence, relative economic gains due to sizable diaspora, active electoral participation as well as a historical-cultural tradition of resisting caste-based inequalities all put together has not been able to pave the way for the rise of any lower castes support based party. Last time BSP could taste success was in the 1997 Assembly elections when it won one seat. The party performance in the Lok Sabha elections has been equally dismal as it has failed to secure even a single seat in the Lok Sabha elections held since 1992.

The failure has essentially been due to the lack of political assertion on the part of the lower castes especially the Scheduled castes community even in Doaba region where they are not only in sizable number but also have the concentrated demographic weight. Cleavages within the Scheduled castes community, as discussed previously, also come in the way of collective voting. Failure of the party high command (read Mayawati) to allow/nurture a state-level leadership, resulting into factionalism, also hurts.[16] Lack of 'winnability factor' is yet another factor that dissuades the electorates to support the party.[17] Inexplicably, despite being a minor party in the state, it last entered into a coalitional arrangement during the 1997 elections even as the Congress has always been open to the idea of an alliance, visibly so in the 2002 and 2007 elections.[18] Also the party has not attempted to build up a cross-caste alliance by nominating candidates from selected castes like in Uttar Pradesh (Wyatt, 2010, p. 187, 190; Chandra, 2004, p. 148). Lack of inner democracy within the party leading to 'representational blockage'[19] also creates fissures as factional fights with tacit encouragement by the party leader plague it.

Related to the marginality issue is the increasing visibility and significance of the Dera[20] in the electoral arena in the state. Recent elections in the state have been witness to the political leaders and candidates cutting across the party lines flocking to Deras seeking blessings and support from the different Dera chiefs, popularly addressed as Guru/Baba/Sant (invariably holy 'men') (Kumar, 2014b).[21] This new-found bonhomie between the political class and the Dera has occurred at a juncture when, symptomatic of a paradigmatic shift in the state politics, religion as a factor for making electoral choices seems to be receding into background with the peace and governance agenda overtook the electoral politics. The shift, first visible during the 1997 Assembly elections, has been evident to the political analysts following the election manifestos/party documents, the campaign and public speeches on the eve of elections (Kumar, 2004; Jodhka, 2000a; Chandhoke and Priyadarshi, 2006). Deras have been depicted in the relevant academic literature as blend of sacred social, cultural, and spiritual spaces of counter-culture.

However, they have also become the potential sites for the mobilisation and assertion for the marginal communities in political/electoral terms as well (Lal, 2009).

In social and cultural terms, how can we explain the mushrooming growth of Deras in the state in the recent decades, and more importantly their rising clout across the state as alternative socio-religious spaces? Why do most of the Dera followers belong to the Scheduled castes or other backward castes, even as many of these Deras are not identified as Scheduled castes Deras and are headed by 'holy men' belonging to high castes/communities? In political/electoral terms, why and how do these different Deras, even the Scheduled castes Deras, seem to be functioning, as of now, in the same way as terrains for low caste mobilisation and recruitment into a manner that facilitates rather than challenges the continued dominance of higher castes/communities? Can Deras, especially the ones identified with the Scheduled castes, credited with culturally empowering role, also be heralding the process of long-awaited 'deepening' of political democracy in the state? The question assumes importance when one considers the fact that not only do the Scheduled castes in the Punjab constitute almost one third of the total electorates, but, compared to their counterparts in other parts of India, they are also relatively better off economically and mobile (Kumar, 2014b).[22]

Arguably, the ever-increasing role of the Deras in influencing political life of their followers, most of whom belong to the socially and economically marginal Punjabis and the migrant low castes farm/industrial labourers from the poorer states of north India, can primarily be attributed to the fact that the social basis of political power has not been effectively challenged and has remained largely unaltered in favour of the dominant castes/communities in the state. As discussed previously, political participation of the marginal castes has remained confined to mere a 'presence' in the party forums or in the legislative bodies, that too thanks to the reservation in the representative bodies. There has hardly been a sincere attempt on the part of either the Congress or BJP or SAD, the three electorally relevant parties in the state, to mobilise the marginal castes/communities for democratic purposes except to secure their vote at the time of elections.[23] Unwilling to share political power yet compelled to seek the crucial support of numerically strong and economically mobile lower castes voters in a closely contested bi-polar polity, the political class takes recourse to 'softer' option of cultivating Deras to 'deliver' en bloc the marginal castes votes. Such a Dera-led 'vote bank' politics resorted to by the parties of all hues is very much in line with the populist/patrimonial mode of politics based on direct 'patronage', 'protection', and 'clientelism' being used recklessly over the years by successive Congress and SAD led political regimes.

It is our argument that the recently attempted 'Dera route' to the mobilisation of Scheduled castes and other backward castes communities for limited electoral purposes is to be understood in the context of the changing trajectory of identity politics in the state as ethnic-regional communal divide has receded into background. The 'route' may ensure better turnout figures among them and possibly also influence their electoral choices, as the political classes/parties seem to have convinced themselves going by their keenness to visit Deras on the eve of elections,[24] but certainly cannot pave the way for their empowerment in substantive terms. Deras are likely to continue to gain in political terms so far as much needed shift in power-terms continue to elude the state. Both SAD and the Congress have not shown any meaningful inclination to put in a mechanism to enable marginal communities to compete for the leadership role.

As of now, Deras have already emerged as the critical centres of counter-culture paving the way for the Scheduled castes' assertion of their recovered values, customs, traditions, self-respect, and pride. They are viewed to have acquired the role of 'the sole and soul spokesmen . . . of the scheduled castes' (Judge and Bal, 2009, p. 106). Are they also emerging as the sites where the 'spiritual and the political are blended dexterously' is a moot question that needs careful exploration as it has long-term implications for the politics of Punjab (Ram, 2012, p. 701). As of now, there does not seem much promise in this regard as the mere presence of Deras is creating social tension. In the past, the attempt on the part of these Dera heads to present themselves as living Guru or even the messenger of God has led to communal violence with the agitated Sikhs on the street. The 2015 incidents of desecration of the Holy Guru Granth Sahib (Adi Granth) in the state were also blamed on the followers of a particular Dera leading to mass agitation.

Determinants of politics

In order to understand the factors that come to play in determining the politics of the state, it is essential to refer to the making of modern Punjab. The remapping of Punjab first in 1947 and then in 1966 made decisive impact over the demographic composition of the state giving rise to new kind of ethnic/communal/caste cleavages as well as other social-political cleavages, like the regional, rural-urban, and caste-class linkages that inform the electoral politics of the state.

In geographical terms, the state underwent the process of territorial reorganisation because of the partition that led to demographic reconfiguration in the aftermath of the communal bloodbath and mass displacement. Loss for the Indian part of Punjab was colossal as it inherited merely 36 percent of the land of undivided Punjab. Eighty percent of the canal-irrigated land along with the cash-rich cotton belt went to the Pakistan part of Punjab. The cropped area in Indian Punjab remained 33 percent as compared to 61 percent in Pakistan part of Punjab. Under the circumstances, the uprooted and dispossessed Sikh landed peasantry received a raw deal. A section of Sikh leadership under the leadership of Master Tara Singh argued that the Sikhs as a community suffered most as they lost their ancestral land. In addition, the Constituent Assembly did not agree to the demand for separate communal representation system in the aftermath of partition. The refusal raised anxiety about the adequacy of representation of the Sikhs in the lawmaking bodies. The community leadership also had to struggle to get the reservation benefits to the Scheduled castes Sikhs (Kumar, 2004).

This sense of victimhood emanating from the community partition experiences continues to linger on. The 'wounded psyche' of the Sikh community, of late, has been expressed in many other forms like the anti-Sikh riots in 1984 and the delay in the punishment to the perpetrators of crime. Radical Sikh elements still make efforts to rekindle it though without much success in order to remain relevant though even moderate. What contributes to it is the 'fairly recent past' of the Sikhs, 'a past heavy with blood and sacrifice' as told in the form of popular history having three sources: Sikh religious texts, sayings and proverbs; and the calendars and other illustrations sold in 'bazaars' (Jeffrey, 1987, p. 59, 62).[25] As a result, Sikh politicians find it 'especially necessary to invoke the past—and to portray past events in a way that did not correspond to any documentary evidence . . . for political purposes'. In fact 'by understanding the dilemma that interaction with their history imposed on Sikh public figures could anyone, government of individual, negotiate fruitfully with Sikhs on matters connected with Punjab politics' (Jeffrey, 1987, p. 59).

The inherited social-political system based on the landed property relationships has continued to play a significant role in determining the politics of the state. The establishment of canal colonies in western central Punjab by the British, because of the legislative measures like the Alienation of Land Act, 1901, provided uniqueness to the social-political structure in an undivided Punjab creating the rural-urban divide between the communities. Only the feudal 'agriculturalist' castes/communities of 'martial race' (the Sikhs and the Muslims) were entitled for the allotment of the land in the canal colonies. 'Non-agriculturalist/trading' communities (mostly Hindus) could not acquire the agricultural land. Colonial policy was to win the abiding loyalty of the politically quiescent peasant castes and communities, whose members constituted almost half of the Indian army, and to strengthen the political and economic dominance of the numerically strong feudal landed peasantry who shared complementarities of interests with the British administrators. 'Punjab tradition' reflected a 'synergy of the authoritarianism of British bureaucrats and the domination of a peasant society by indigenous landlords' (Stern, 2001, p. 50).

British administration made a deliberate attempt to insulate the rural masses in the state from the urban populace, as it was keen that the nationalist forces led by the Congress could not extend its influence. Hindu upper castes traditionally dominated trade, commerce and service sectors in urban Punjab. Lack of business/industrial establishment served the imperial interests as the rural youth saw the military service as the only viable employment avenue in the absence of any alternative. The prominence of state parties like Punjab National Unionist Party, a party of landed peasantry (called

Vadheras) was testimony of the feudal dominance in rural Punjab, which was friendly to the imperial interests (Ahsan, 2005, p. 98).[26]

In social terms, Punjab has been a medley of religious, ethnic, linguistic, and caste groups. As mentioned previously, the complex nature of the electoral politics of Punjab can be attributed to the presence of several societal factors like caste, religion, and language (script also) that combine together to determine political contours of the state. Punjab has had a 'culture and language, which transcends religious group boundaries' though politics had its adverse impact in creating divisions (Kumar, Pramod, 2014, p. 220). The British reinforced and constructed inter-community competitiveness in the political arena by introducing separate communal electorate. The Hindu-Sikh relationship has been contentious at times after the exodus of Muslims from Indian part of Punjab. The demographic configuration underwent a change after the exodus of Muslims in the aftermath of the partition having its impact over the electoral politics of the state. The percentage of Hindus increased from 28 percent to 64 percent, whereas the percentage of the Sikhs in the overall population also increased from 13 percent to 33 percent. Significantly, in the Punjabi-speaking part of the post-partition Punjab, Sikhs constituted the majority in 8 out of 12 districts (Sarhadi, 1970, p. 152). After the reorganisation of the state on linguistic basis in 1966, the Sikhs in Punjab became a majority. The Hindus accounted for only 37 percent. This led to a situation in which

> both the Hindus and Sikhs continued to suffer from a minority persecution complex but with a difference . . . the Hindus suffered from a majority-minority complex as they perceived themselves to be majority in India but a minority in reorganised Punjab; the Sikhs for their part were perceived to have a minority-majority complex, as majority in Punjab and a minority in India.
>
> (Kumar, Pramod, 2014, p. 223)

As for the other bases of the assertion of identity politics, mention should be specifically made of language and script. If the Urdu-Hindi divide marked the nature pre-partition politics, then the Punjabi-Hindi divide marked the communalisation of the language issue in post-partition Punjab. In the successive census held after partition, a large number of Hindus under the influence of the Hindu organisations like Arya Samaj declared Hindi and not Punjabi as their mother language. Interestingly, there were still others ready to accept Punjabi as their language only if it was in Devnagari rather than Gurmukhi script. The Sikh community during the Punjabi Suba movement identified Punjabi in Gurmukhi script, as it was in Gurmukhi in which the Sikh Holy Scripture Guru Granth Sahib (Adi Granth) was compiled.

To sum up, societal factors like religion, caste, region, and language (and script) have combined differently in different elections in reorganised Punjab to produce contrasting electoral outcomes. Despite efforts to articulate a 'composite linguistic-cultural consciousness' in the post-partition Punjab, it could not lead to the development of a 'unified sub-nationality with a common political goal' (Kumar, 2014b, p. 220). At the same time, operating under the same administrative and political setup for a considerable period of time has made it possible for the parties, even the ones starkly different from each other in ideological terms, to 'come together' and make the coalitional mode of politics work as witnessed in case of the SAD and BJP.

Notes

1 In neighbouring Haryana, administrative districts have turned in to electoral units revealing distinct electoral trends as well and leadership.
2 Majha region has three parliamentary constituencies namely Gurdaspur, Amritsar, and Khadur Sahib. Doaba region comprises of Jalandhar and Hoshiarpur (both seats are reserved for the SC candidates). Malwa region comprises of Anandpur Sahib, Fatehgarh Sahib, Ludhiana, Patiala, Sangrur, Faridkot, Ferozpur, and Bathinda (Fatehgarh Sahib and Faridkot seats are reserved for the SC Candidates).
3 It was in Majha region, considered to be the 'cradle of Sikhism' due to the presence of main Sikh shrines and pilgrimage centres associated with the Sikh Gurus in the region where the autonomist movement gained ground before spreading to Doaba and Malwa region (Deol, 2000, p. 2).
4 The core of Anandpur Sahib Resolution veered round two main demands: one, recognition of the Sikh community constituting as a distinct nation (Qaum); and two, the autonomy of the constituent states *vis-à-vis* the centre (Singh, 2007, pp. 559–60).
5 In recent years, the ruling parties in Gujarat, Bihar, Madhya Pradesh, Orissa, Chhattisgarh, and Andhra Pradesh have managed to defy anti-incumbency factor for considerable period of time.
6 In neighbouring Haryana, the first time an incumbent party was able to retain power in its electoral history was in the 2009 elections when the Congress was able to form a minority government in alliance with now defunct Janhit Congress.
7 Chandra (2004) dubs BSP and SAD as 'ethnic parties'.
8 The overall turnout in the Assembly elections across the states in India touched around 70 percent, up from around 60 percent in the 1990s. There has also been a substantial narrowing of the gender gap in the voter turnout and an upsurge in the turnout among Scheduled castes and Scheduled tribes.
9 India's electoral system has in recent years become increasingly 'subaltern friendly' as it has 'given the members of subaltern groups a point of entry into ruling elite and a share of state resources' Chandra (2012).
10 Scheduled castes constitute 31.9 percent of the state's population as per the 2011 census, highest in the country. However, Scheduled castes are divided not only along the caste lines but also religious lines that result in 'an absence of any visible pattern in their voting behaviour' (Judge, 2012, p. 18). There are 39 Scheduled castes and the two most numerous castes are Chamars and Churas. Chamars have either remained Hindu or have identified them as Ramdasias or Adi-dharmis.
11 Increasing entrenchment of political power in the hands of the wealthy and influential political families, more often than not interrelated in prudent marriage alliances, that belong mostly to the dominant landed Jat Sikh community leaves hardly any scope for the Congress and the Akali Dal leadership which come from the same stock to encourage the empowerment of the subaltern communities in electoral terms of contestation and representation. Democracy as a self-correcting mechanism does not seem to be working in the state as for now.
12 Underlining the rural-urban divide between the two religious communities, in rural Punjab Sikhs are around 70 percent and Hindus around 29 percent,

whereas in the urban Punjab the Hindus are around 66 percent and Sikhs are around 31 percent (Corsi, 2006, p. 94)

13 Around 27 percent of the total number of Indian army recruits (around 800,000) during the Second World War was recruited from Punjab. Sikhs had participated also in large number in the First World War. Almost all the recruits were from the 'martial castes/communities', the ones favoured by the Act, 1901 (Talbot, 1980, p. 75).

14 Such a measure was undertaken in Madhya Pradesh under Digvijay Singh led Congress government in the 1990s, costing his party the support of upper and middle castes.

15 If during militancy, a sizable number of militants belonged to the Scheduled castes landless Sikhs, it was also due to the existing structures of inequality that fuelled their resentment (Purewal, 2000).

16 Since 1999, the party has been divided into three 'Bahujan' parties, namely, the BSP, the BSP (Ambedkar) and Democratic Bahujan Samaj Morcha (DBSM).

17 Chhibber and Murali (2006, pp. 5–6) have argued that 'two partyism' dominates elections to the state assemblies in India. They attribute it to 'strategic voting'— 'voters prefer not to waste their votes if meaningful and consequential votes can be cast'.

18 BSP is often accused of playing the role of a spoiler for the Congress as it is credited with weaning away the lower castes votes which otherwise would go to the Congress. The Congress losing from Gurdaspur and Hoshiarpur constituencies in the 2019 election was partly attributed to BSP doing well in some pockets.

19 Based on her field study of Hoshiarpur, Kanchan Chandra has attributed the failure of BSP to the fact that the numerically strong Balmiki community does not extend its wholehearted support due to the Jatav community dominated leadership of the party in the state (Chandra, 2004, p. 22).

20 Dera followers belong to a religious sect that is often 'an offshoot of an established religion'. They share 'common beliefs . . . including some novel concepts distinct from the mother religion'. A Dera as such 'may reject some norms existing in the mainstream religion and replace obsolete elements with new practices' (Lal, 2009, p. 224).

21 Every Dera is headed by a Guru who confers 'the benefits of sacred learning on human beings and acts as an advisor to those who seek spiritual guidance' (Lal, 2009, p. 224). These gurus/babas are revered by their followers either as messengers of god or spiritual teachers. In Sikhism, the term 'Guru' means 'remover of darkness' and is reserved only for revered Guru Granth Sahib (Adi Granth). The terms 'Vahiguru' as well as 'Satguru' stand for God, the divine preceptor (Nesbitt, 2010, pp. 3–4).

22 Breakdown of colonial structure of *Jajmani* or *balutedari* relations in the wake of the Green Revolution meant that family ties between landed and landless families that provided a cushion to an exploitative binding feudal relationship disappeared, replaced by market relationship.

23 Parties belonging to *Sanjha Morcha* with their largely upper castes leadership skirted the caste question.

24 Since politicians do visit many public places during their campaign so why to give such significance to their Dera visits? Visits to different Deras by star campaigners during the crucial week before the polling date is sufficient evidence of their conviction about the crucial role these Deras play in determining the electoral choices.

25 While presenting a 'panoramic view' of Sikh history, Singh (2007, p. 555) argues in a comparative sense that any community resorting to 'violence or non-violence (is) determined by its strategic perspectives to achieve (its) politico-economic goals and not from any doctrinal adherence to violence or non-violence'.

26 Ahsan (2005, p. 98).

3 Politics of colonial Punjab

This chapter focuses on the politics of colonial Punjab from the vantage point of Shiromani Akali Dal (SAD), the oldest surviving state-level party in India, which has been instrumental in effecting the paradigmatic changes/development in the politics of Punjab. This would more be the case after state underwent reorganisation twice, first in 1947 and then in 1966, both times religion playing a major role. The 'panthic' party was formed on 20 December 1920 following the formation of Shiromani Gurdwara Prabhandhak Committee (SGPC). On 14 December 1920, a meeting of the Akali Jathas (congregation), constituted for the purpose of gurdwara reforms movement, took place at Amritsar where the decision was taken to set up SAD. The word 'Akali' is derived from the word 'Akal' which has its origin from the Sanskrit word Kal (time). Thus 'Akal' literally means the one who 'does not die' and belongs to the immortal/God. The term 'Akali' was first used by Sikh tenth Guru, Guru Gobind Singh, for those of his followers who were prepared to sacrifice even their lives for the protection of panth (Kumar and Kaur, 2019).

At the time of its formation, the party acted as an institutional-political arm of the SGPC. As political arm of the SGPC, it was originally tasked with the aim to lead the movement to bring about reforms in the gurdwaras. The SAD was to have four declared objectives: to bring the Sikh religious places under Panthic control, to do away with the institution of Mahants, to utilise the property and income of the gurdwaras for the purpose for which they were founded, and to practice the Sikh religion according to the teachings of the Sikh Gurus as enshrined in the Guru Granth Sahib (Adi Granth) (Singh, Ajit, 2005, p. 32). SAD was set up with four objectives in mind: a) to bring the Sikh religious places under panthic control; b) to do away with the entrenched position of the Mahants, thus ending their irresponsibility; c) to utilise the property and income of the gurdwara for the purpose for which they were founded; and d) to practice the Sikh religion according to the teachings of the Sikh Gurus as enshrined in the Adi-Granth (Singh, 2005, p. 32).

In its formative years, the party actively assisted the Sikh community in its effort to free the gurdwaras from the clutches of Hindu Mahants and bring all of them under the supervision of the SGPC by mobilising the Sikh community. The agenda was also to restore the Sikh tradition of worship in the Sikh gurdwaras, as there was an opposition to certain religious practices being allowed in the gurdwaras by the mahants not in tenor with the Sikh maryada, who were also seen as corrupt and in league with the colonial masters (Kumar and Kaur, 2019).

Despite the popular sentiment for reforms, mahants having tacit support of the British were not ready to leave the control of the gurdwaras. Only a few mahants voluntarily gave up the control of the gurdwaras to the SAD leadership (Grewal, 1996, p. 34). The SAD leadership launched many morchas. Jathas comprising of the Akali cadres were sent to occupy the control of gurdwaras. They faced repressive action by both the private armies of the mahants and the imperial police. The movement led to the forcible 'liberation' of over 300 large and small gurdwaras (Adi Granth) (Singh, Mohinder, 1988, p. 19). The British finally relented and the Gurdwara Act was passed on 1 November 1925. According to the Act, all the important Sikh gurdwaras were placed legally under the control of the SGPC. Local gurdwaras were to have their own elected bodies for management of the shrines with one nomine on its committee (Singh, Ajit, 2005, p. 26). SGPC emerged as 'a sort of parliament' of Sikhs. SGPC decisions

> acquired the sanctity of the ancient Gurmata, . . . and the income from gurdwaras . . . gave it financial sustenance . . . disbursement of this income in the management of shrines, patronage in the appointment of hundreds of Granthis, Sevadars (temple servants) teachers and professors for schools and colleges which were built, arrangements for the training of Granthis and for missionary activity outside the Punjab, all made the (SGPC) . . . a government within the government.
>
> (Singh, Khuswant, 1977, pp. 213–14)

The gurdwara reform movement was significant not only in establishing SAD as the foremost Sikh political organisation, but it also had a wider national impact: first, it created a sense of confidence among Indians that British could be forced to meet their genuine demands through non-violent mass movement, an idea that was already put to practice by Gandhi during the non-cooperation movement in the early 1920s; second, it brought SAD and Congress leadership close to each other resulting into an intensification in the nationalist movement in the state; third, SGPC-SAD combine provided an institutional and organisational structure to respond to the social and political aspirations of the Sikh community. Along with the Akal Takht, it became the pillars of Sikh politics.

The SGPC and the SAD since their inceptions as two pillars of the Sikh politics have always been closely linked to the Punjab politics as it has unfolded at least up until the time of this writing. While the supremacy of the SGPC in the religious affairs was established after the movement success, the SAD became the leading political organisation of the Sikhs (Tutleja, 1984, p. 123). To underline the role of the SGPC in the faction-ridden SAD, only the party faction which wins majority of seats in the SGPC election is always considered by people as the 'official' Akali Dal. Due to its access to the gurdwara workers, Sikh organisations, and resources, the SGPC has remained the most important non-government bureaucratic organisation and the pre-eminent institution of the Sikh community, dubbed as a 'state within a state' (Brass, 1974, p. 311; Puri, 1995, p. 35; Nayar, 1968, p. 77).

The Akali confrontation with the British during the reform movement, though dubbed as non-political, did politicise and mobilise the Sikh community on the basis of religion and brought the panthic issues to the core of Punjab politics in the years to come. Thus after the success of gurdwara reform movement, the party aimed now to secure adequate political representation to the Sikh community in the evolving democratic institutions of colonial India at that time. Entry into the mainstream electoral politics seeking political power for the Sikhs as a separate ethnic entity was a natural progression as the SAD had always considered itself as the political mouthpiece of the Sikhs and also tasked with the noble cause of reviving the old spirit and glory of the Sikh Panth. The party was helped by the colonial policy of dividing Indians into Sikh, Muslim, and general categories for electoral purposes in the name of safeguarding the interests of the minorities and allowing them separate communal representation.

The immediate triggering factor for SAD joining electoral battle was the community dissatisfaction with the inadequate share of representation given to them in the Punjab Legislative Council under Montague-Chelmsford Scheme (Tutleja, 1984, p. 135). Muslims had secured 50 percent of the non-official seats of the Council. In continuity with the demand raised by the Chief Khalsa Diwan (CKD), the SAD demanded a 30 percent share of representation for the Sikhs in the Punjab Legislative Council and also in the Central Legislative Assembly in case its demand for the abolition of the communal representation, based on the theory of the separate electorates, was not accepted. Simon Commission, set up in November 1927, to review the working of the constitutional reforms of 1919 by the British government was boycotted by the SAD (like the Congress) on the grounds that it had no Indian member. However, the contentious issue like the demand by the Congress for the dominion status and not full-fledged independence raised considerable resentment among the Akalis. Baba Kharak Singh termed the dominion status as equivalent to 'semi-slavery' and asked Sikhs not to participate in the civil disobedience movement, though he was opposed by another influential Akali leader, Master Tara Singh (Kumar and Kaur, 2019).

The Simon Commission in its report recommended the continuation of the separate communal electorate and reservation of seats in the legislative bodies. In the case of Punjab, the Commission took the position that it was impossible to concede 30 percent reservation for the Sikhs, given their numerical proportion in the overall population (15 percent). On 12 February 1928, the Congress called an all parties conference in Delhi to discuss the formulation of a constitutional proposal for India which was participated in by the SAD. The resultant Nehru Committee Report, 1928, recommended the abolition of a separate communal representation, considering it detrimental to the unity of India and urged the introduction of the secular joint electorate for all religious communities. However, it agreed to make an exception in the case of the Muslim community on the grounds that their relative economic and education backwardness would come in the way of their effective representation in the legislative bodies. The SAD leadership rejected this recommendation and demanded the complete abolition of communal representation by the British in Punjab and all over India. The Akali position was that if communal representation was to be given to any minority then the same concession was to be extended to the Sikh minority in the Punjab as well. The first round table Conference which was held in 1930 included the representatives of every community and every organisation in India including the representatives from the princely states, expect the Indian National Congress. Though the Central Sikh League refused to participate in it, the moderate Sikh leaders, i.e. Ujjal Singh and Sampuran Singh, represented the Sikh community at the conference. The Sikh representatives presented a memorandum asking for the same treatment (30 percent reservation in the legislative bodies) in Punjab as the Muslim minority had received in other provinces where they had sizable presence. Ramsay McDonald announced the communal award in 1932. Seat distribution remained in the favour of the Muslims who were given 86 out of 175 seats in the Punjab Legislative Assembly whereas 33 out of 175 seats were reserved for the Sikhs. In the North-West Frontier Legislative Council, 3 out of 50 seats were reserved for the Sikhs. In the federal Legislative Assembly, 6 out of 250 seats and in the council of states 4 out of 150 seats were reserved for the community (Singh, Ajit, 2005, pp. 28–30). The communal award was rejected by the miffed SAD leadership as a 'scrap of paper' to be 'buried' along with the Nehru and Simon Commission Report (Tutleja, 1984, p. 151). The Sikh leadership also complained that by accepting universal adult suffrage, the Nehru committee had attempted to establish Muslim rule in Punjab as Muslims commanded a numerical majority in the Punjab province. Baba Kharak Singh expressed his anguish by resigning from the Congress and exhorted the Sikhs to throw the Nehru Report into the 'dustbin'. Despite the inter-party bitterness, the SAD leadership consented to the dual membership and also agreed to contest the 1937 election in an alliance with the Congress (Narang, 2014, p. 340). The making of the alliance could be explained in the opposition of the two parties towards the Unionist Party which enjoyed the support of the powerful landed peasantry and was viewed as collaborating with the British government. In the 1937 elections, the Unionist Party secured the majority by getting 96 out of 175 seats of Punjab Legislative Assembly. The Congress obtained 18 seats and the Muslim League got only two. Among the Sikhs, Khalsa National Party, considered moderate, won 18 out of 33 seats reserved for the Sikh community in the Assembly (Kapoor, 1986, p. 52). With the absolute majority of the Unionist Party in the Legislative Assembly, Sir Sikander Hayat Khan formed a ministry in the Punjab, joined by Sunder Singh Majithia belonging to the CKD in the cabinet. Only one urban non-agriculturist Hindu was included in the cabinet, underlining the hold of the rural landed peasantry over the politics of Punjab (Singh, Khuswant, 1977, p. 234).

More than the Unionist Party, the SAD was opposed to the Muslim League, as it perceived the Muslims having a disproportionate share of power in the state legislative body. While it saw Muslim League as a communal party, it was willing to have truck with the Unionist Party, a secular party having a support base among all religious communities (Narang, 2014, p. 340). It was under pressure from the Akali leadership that the Congress modified its stand by drafting a resolution which stated that the Congress would not accept any constitutional setup which did not give equal and fair treatment to all minorities, particularly to the Sikhs (Gulati, 1977, p. 50). However, the gap between the SAD and the Congress gradually widened as the Congress had a support base among the Sikhs also. The party was also not seen as fully supportive of the Akali demands (Kumar and Kaur, 2019).

Following the Montague-Chelmsford Reforms, 1919, which introduced communal electorate, the SAD became involved in ensuring fair representation of the Sikh community into legislative bodies and in the public services. The Passage of the Government of India Act, 1935, led to the establishment of the provincial legislative assemblies in British India. SAD contested the 1937 elections on its own, hoping to corner the Sikh votes for the seats reserved for the Sikh community. The Unionist party, enjoying the support in rural Punjab with the help of both Muslim and Sikh landlords, secured a majority by getting 96 out of 175 seats of Punjab provincial legislative assembly. Congress won 18 seats whereas the Muslim League got only two seats, though it won 75 out of 85 seats reserved for Muslims in the subsequent 1946 provincial legislative Assembly elections, showing the growing clout of the party rooting for the partition of the country on the basis of two-nation theory (Talbot, 1980, p. 65). It changed the political scenario of undivided Punjab as till then the Unionist party (also called Zamindara party) had dominated the party system in the state. The parties in favour of united India sought an alliance with it to share power in the state. Like the Unionist party, in the pre-partition period, SAD was controlled by the feudal landed peasantry. It was only during the gurdwara movement and for a short period after that the radical peasant forces had the leadership for a brief period. Resenting it, the feudal elements had formed rival Central Akali Dal in 1934 (Alam, 1986, p. 21). Sikhs in the 1937 elections had voted for the moderate Khalsa National Party, founded in 1936, as the party was able to win 18 out of 33 seats reserved for the Sikhs (Kapur, 1986, p. 52). The Congress party did not enjoy much support, as it was the Unionist party that represented the powerful landed peasantry cutting across the religious divide and enjoying the colonial regime patronage. The SAD relation with the Congress came under strain during the Second World War as the Akalis refused to support the Congress call to boycott the call for fresh recruitment in the British army (Verma, 1987, p. 267). The party also did not join the Quit India movement, though a faction jointly led by Giani Gurmukh Singh Musafir, Partap Singh

Kairon, Darshan Singh Pheruman, Udham Singh Nagoke, among others, supported it and offered themselves for arrest (Nayar, 1968, p. 81).

It was in their opposition to the demand for Pakistan by the Muslim League in March 1940 at its annual conference in Lahore, which brought the Congress and the SAD closer as both parties opposed the partition (Singh, Ajit, 2005, p. 34). Condemning the resolution for a separate Muslim state, Master Tara Singh in his letter, dated 1 May 1942 to Stafford Cripps made it clear that the Sikhs and the Hindus of Punjab did not want to go out of India (Verma, 1987, p. 269). In their opposition to the idea of Pakistan, the Sikh leaders did not hesitate even to share the platform with the leaders of the Hindu Mahasabha which stood for India as a single political unit as one Rashtra/Akhand Bharat. The partition proposal had raised apprehension among the SAD leadership, rightly so, about the future of the Sikhs. Conscious of the presence of the sizable Sikh community settled in the western part of Punjab especially in the canal colonies and scattered in other parts of eastern Punjab, Akalis feared the loss of land and migration, an apprehension which was proven true. To thwart the Muslim League design, however, the SAD even proposed unsuccessfully the 'Azad Punjab scheme' having the mixed population of Punjabi-speaking people belonging to different religions (Narang, 2014, p. 341).

The provincial elections outcome in 1946 reflected the now entrenched communal divides that marked the state as the Muslim League succeeded in winning 75 seats reserved for the Muslims. SAD was able to win 22 seats whereas the Congress, despite its secular credentials, could win majority of Hindu seats only (40 out of 51). The once dominant Unionist party could now win only 20 seats that too in rural Punjab only as the party continued to retain support among the influential landlords. In the case of a fractured verdict, the SAD entered into an alliance with the Unionist party and the Congress to form the coalition government after its talks with the Muslim League failed over the Akali demand of reserving 25 percent of the cabinet positions and also the government posts for the Sikhs. As the 1946 Cabinet Mission proposals were accepted by both the Congress and the Muslim League and partition loomed large on the horizon, the SAD made a last ditch effort to have an understanding with the Muslim League as it was apprehensive about the future of the Sikhs living in the Muslim-majority western Punjab. However, talks with Jinnah failed and then the Akalis threw their lot with the Congress and its promise of a secular India where minority rights would be protected. The SAD, however, refused to join the Constituent Assembly in protest as the Congress refused to support the separate communal electorate though the Sikhs from the Congress party did join (Narang, 2014, p. 341).

At the time of its inception and for a longer period of its career the SAD retained its original character of being a 'movement'-oriented cadre-based party with panthic ideology. During the entire pre-independence period, as discussed previously, the Akali politics was engaged in the battle for 'representation' through the mechanism of either sectarian communal representation or of self-determination, which continued even after partition. In spatial terms, SAD despite the dominance of the Unionist Party received its support from rural Punjab. In community terms, the support came mainly from the Sikh peasant community though the party leadership came from urban middle class. The Muslim League increased its support base among Muslims in the decade before partition due to the growing communalisation of the state politics. Its gains were evident in the 1946 provincial elections.

4 Politics of Punjab after partition

Partition meant that colonial Punjab lost two-thirds of the territory and half of its population to Pakistan. State reorganisation in 1966 resulted in a further loss of more than half of the territory of the post-partition Punjab (Akbar, 1985, pp. 155–6). Changing demography of the state was a crucial factor in shaping the Akali politics in the post-partition period. In pre-partition Punjab, Muslims constituted half of the population. Indian Punjab after partition, however, was made up of over 60 percent Hindu population and 31 percent Sikh population. Besides the increased percentage of Sikhs in post-partition Punjab, the Sikh community got territorially concentrated in central Punjab due to heavy migration from now what was part of Pakistan. The historically evolved communal divide between the two communities in post-partition India may be viewed either as 'a manifestation of a deep-rooted economic divide which became accentuated after the green revolution of the 1960s' or as a 'spill over of a power struggle between the two principal political parties in Punjab, Congress and the Akali Dal' (Sharma, 1986, p. 634).

The post-partition period witnessed the Akali demand for separate Punjabi Suba. Because of the demographic shift and territorial reconfiguration, the dual strategy of SAD leadership to fight for both reforms within the community and political representation receded into the background as it emerged now as an electoral party seeking political power. As discussed in the preceding section, partition and resulting communal bloodbath had witnessed the rise of anti-Muslims sentiment and Hindu-Sikh unity. Cleavage happened after the exodus of Muslims, making Indian Punjab essentially a dual-community province. The partition resulted in the leftover Hindu and the Sikh communities competing for political and economic supremacy in the truncated state. The rural-urban divide also played a role as Hindus were mostly urban-based, whereas the Sikhs were mainly rural residents.

Demand for the creation of Punjabi Suba contributed a great deal in shaping the contemporary Sikh identity. Though the Punjabi Suba movement was launched ostensibly on the linguistic basis, the Akali leadership never concealed its real intention either, which was to have a 'territorial homeland' for the Sikh community (Lamba, 1999). The Sikhs led by the Akali leadership asserted their distinct ethnic identity in cultural terms. The Akali leadership demanded the reorganisation of post-partition Punjab on a linguistic basis and not on a communal basis. In a comparative mode, the movement asking for the reorganisation of Punjab on a linguistic basis is to be viewed within the wider context of the nationwide movement of linguistic groups seeking statehood as well as the assertion of the demand for a 'self-determined political status' for the Sikhs within the union (Anand, 1976, p. 263).[1]

Hindu-Sikh distinctions came to the forefront more prominently than ever once the agitation for a separate Punjabi Suba began. It was manifested in the rejection of Punjabi as their language by a sizable number of non-Sikhs during 1961 census. Also the State Reorganisation Commission, formed by the centre to recommend the formation of linguistic states, considered Punjabi as a dialect rather than a language and rejected the demand for Punjabi Suba. Both these developments were viewed by the sizable Sikh population as 'an overt and deliberate political act designed to undercut linguistic basis of Punjabi Suba demand'. The Hindu majority, Brass argues, in its inability to assimilate the Sikhs 'adopted the tactic of avoiding their language so that the Sikhs, a minority people by religion, might become a minority by language as well' (Brass, 1974, p. 327, 298). The Hindu-Sikh divide was evident in the conflicting assertions about what should be the script of Punjabi, Gurumukhi or Devnagari (Sarhadi, 1970, p. 211). The rural-urban divide also played a role in keeping the divide simmering.

Notably, during the Punjabi Suba movement, there was a significant change in the social composition of the party leadership. Until the 1950s, the Akali leadership came from the urban upper caste middle-class Sikhs while the majority of the Sikhs lived in rural Punjab. The widening and deepening of democracy in an electoral sense with each passing decade, along with the economic empowerment of the landowning Jat Sikh community in the wake of the Green Revolution, transformed the leadership structure within Akali Dal. The movement witnessed a qualitative shift in the social origin of the Akali leadership as it now came primarily from the rural Jat-Sikh background. The support base of Akalis, as earlier discussed, always came mainly from the Sikhs residing in rural Punjab. The change in the leadership profile was symbolised by the emergence of Sant Fateh Singh, a Jat Sikh in the place of Master Tara Singh, an elite caste urban-based Khatri, described as 'Bhapa' by rural folks and a representative of urban Sikhs (Bajwa, 1979, p. 25). Since then Jat Sikhs, numerically strong and landowning peasant caste, have dominated the party leadership. Significantly, the emergence of Sant Fateh Singh, who was from Malwa region, also led the gradual shift of the Akali Leadership base from the Doaba and Majha region to Malwa region. Until then the prominent Akali leaders—like Giani Kartar Singh, Master Tara Singh, Udham Singh Nagoke, Giani Bhupinder Singh—all belonged to Doaba and Majha regions.

Dominance of the Jat Sikh community within the SAD and also the Congress[2] considerably weakened the political role of other castes among the Sikhs, which were earlier influential namely mercantile upper castes Khatris, Aroras, and Ahulwalias. The same fate awaited the hitherto dormant artisan castes, like the Tarkhans or the Ramgarhias (carpenter and ironworkers), Chimbas (tailors), and Kumhars (potters), and the Scheduled castes, like the Chamars (tanners) and Chuhras or Balmikis (sweepers), also called Mazhabis and Ramdasias, thus creating internal cleavages within the Sikh community. The fact that Punjab has a very large proportion of Scheduled castes, including the Scheduled castes Sikhs (Majhabis), has further added to the sharpness of these cleavages (Jodhka, 2000b, p. 392).

Sikh community is not a homogeneous community as it consists of different castes. There are important differences within the community along class and regional lines that have increased in the aftermath of the Green Revolution, which disproportionately helped the large landholding Sikh peasantry of Malwa region (Puri, 1995, p. 49). Politically, economically, and numerically, Jats—and, after 1966, Sikh Jats—have been the single most important social group at the village level. Community's ascendance to political dominance as reflected in the social profile of the party leadership can be attributed to three factors: first, the community has been the foremost landowning community in the state. Capital-intensive and market-oriented Green Revolution with its 'betting on the strong policy' helped primarily the rich farmers who had large land holdings. It gradually led to a situation of greater landlessness in the state as rich farmers started purchasing the lands of the small and marginal farmers. Second, in electoral terms, the community has the demographic weight, constituting 20 to 30 percent of the state's population. Third, the community is considered as elite caste despite not being 'twice-born' caste. It has been helped by the fact that due to the reformist movement like the Bhakti movement, Sufism, Ad-dharm movement, and influence of Sikhism, caste-based hierarchy is not as strong as in other north Indian states. Also, the legacy of Maharaja Ranjit Singh who established the Sikh empire, followed by princely rulers all belonging to Jat Sikh community, has added to the status of the caste.

The overwhelming importance of Jat Sikhs in the political leadership has been visible in SAD and also in the Congress.[3] This becomes evident if we refer to the sociological origins of the lawmakers, elected from the state. Out of 1,248 Legislative assembly members elected from the state from 1967 to 2012, a sizable 44 percent of them belonged to Jat Sikh community whereas Khatris/Aroras constituted 22 percent. That left the OBC MLAs at only 9 percent. Since there has been reservation for the Scheduled castes (right now, it is 34 out of 117 seats after the fourth delimitation exercise, before the exercise it was only 29), so their representation remains assured. However, Scheduled castes candidates have not been able to win from unreserved seats nor do the main parties in the state show a keenness to allot tickets to them (Kumar, Pramod, 2014, p. 307).

Politics of electoral alliances

As discussed previously, it was only after the partition and the decline/oblivion of the Unionist Party as well as the Muslim League and also under the single plurality secular electoral system based on universal franchise that the Congress party could manage to emerge as the winnable party in the state.[4] Even the efforts on the part of SAD to mobilise social support on the Punjabi Suba issue could get the party only 19 seats with only 11.7 percent of the vote. In 1952 Assembly elections, SAD had won 33 seats and 14.7 percent of the vote. In 1956 elections, SAD had merged with the Congress in the hope of the central government allowing the creation of Sikh majority Punjabi Suba. After disillusionment on this count, the Akali leadership opted out of the Congress. However, many Akali MLAs who had joined the Congress government refused to resign. It was therefore a much weakened party which had its dismal performance in the 1962 Assembly elections. BJS, the other electorally relevant party, fighting alone managed to increase its seat tally gradually because of the growing Hindu-Sikh divide on the Punjabi Suba issue. The party won nine seats in the 1962 elections, up from two seats in 1952 elections (Kumar, 2004, 2007).

Even after reorganisation of the state with a Sikh majority, SAD could get only one-fifth votes and 24 seats in the assembly of 104 members in the 1967 Assembly elections. Not only the reorganised state had a sizable Hindu community but also a sizable segment of Sikh voters still supported the Congress. SAD won 43 and 58 seats in 1969 and 1977 assembly elections, respectively, which was an improvement in the panthic party's electoral fortunes but not sufficient to capture power. BJS also gained marginally in reorganised state as party was viewed as supportive of trading and business classes interests in an agrarian economy. The party also represented itself as the saviour of the minority Hindu community political interests. What was common between BJS and SAD was that both contested on the plank of 'anti-Congressism'. BJS merged with the Janata Party and contested the 1977 elections in alliance with SAD. The coalition victory in 1977 was both due to their complementary support base as well as for the party workers' active resistance against the emergency. Significantly, even when the Congress got merely 17 seats in this election, it polled at 33.6 percent of votes polled, higher than 31.4 percent of vote polled by SAD, thus confirming the stable support base of the Congress.[5]

Almost all contestant parties in the assembly elections held particularly after the reorganisation have shown inclination to enter in to alliances—pre- or post-electoral. Many of these alliances were short-lived and opportunistic and not ideological. While SAD entered into alliance with BJS and then with the Janata Party in different elections before it fired up its alliance with the BJP in 1997, the Congress entered into long-term alliance with the CPI, which continued until 2002 assembly elections. Other minor short-lived parties have invariably sought to challenge the entrenched parties by forging alliances. Most recently, SAD (Taksali)-Punjab Ekta Party entered in to alliance in 2019 elections.

Compulsion for the Congress to enter into electoral alliance was two fold. First, Congress wanted to broaden its support base to rural Punjab to counter Akali advantage and second, it wanted to strengthen its image as a secular party by entering into alliance with the Communist parties, which had support base among the Sikh rural peasantry of Punjab especially in the Malwa region. However, the Congress never inducted its electoral ally as partner in the government.

As for SAD, its leadership long realised that reorganisation was not going to ensure an electoral majority in party's favour. The realisation occurred as the party failed to get a majority in the newly created Punjab state. This was contrary to the expectation of the party, as Akalis had thought of securing Sikh majority votes. The party discovered to its dismay that the Congress not only put up an impressive number of Sikh candidates but also continued to enjoy a decent support base both among Sikhs and Hindus. This became one of the factors as to why SAD started looking for an alliance in order to take on the Congress. Projecting itself as a secular party, holding the middle ideological ground, Congress claimed to represent interests of both communities. Congress thus effectively 'cut off the support base of all other political parties, instead of seeking to accommodate them' (Sharma, 1986, p. 640).

Despite making a strident and conscious effort to assert its panthic identity, SAD could come to power only by aligning with BJS. The SAD-BJS (now BJP) alliance appeared 'natural' in the sense that their respective social support bases are complementary. Unlike the rural Sikh support base of SAD, BJS' support base was limited to the urban constituencies among upper-caste Hindus.

Coalitional politics in the state has also been helped by the fact that Majha, Doaba and Malwa are primarily geographical/historical/cultural regions and there is no dominance of any particular caste or community as it is Jat Sikhs who dominate all the three regions. At the constituency level, the 1971 delimitation exercise which remapped the territorial boundaries of the constituencies witnessed Sikh majority rural segments getting merged with the Hindu majority urban ones.[6]

The SAD-BJS alliance set the pattern of sharing of power between the representatives of the two communities to strike a social balance, which neither of the two parties could establish on its own. Failure to win power on its own compelled Akalis to sustain the politics of identity even after the reorganisation of the state. The steamroller majority of the Congress in the 1972 assembly elections further contributed to this sense of hurt and stoked the fires of identity politics. The Akali leadership continued to project itself as protector of the Punjabi language as well as the Sikh religion as against the deliberate pursuit of the policy to assimilate/accommodate the language and culture of a minority group. The SAD leadership realised that the party could come to power on its own only in an exceptional situation like when the voting takes place on sharp communal line, as in the 1985 elections. Moreover, even in the case of winning electoral majority on its own, there would always be a question mark about the panthic party's legitimacy to rule over a state where Hindus are only marginally less than half of the population. That explains why even after securing clear majority in the assembly elections held in 1997, the SAD still chose to form a coalition government with the BJP.

Going back, elections held in 1967 after reorganisation gave an early indication about the rural-urban, regional as well as religious divides in the state influencing the electoral choices of people. To illustrate the point, reference can be made of the social profile of the elected representatives in the Legislative Assembly constituted in 1967 after the reorganisation of the state (Kumar and Sharma, 2009a). SAD was able to win its majority of seats (18 out of 35 seats won) from rural constituencies in Malwa region. Around 67 percent of Akali legislators were from rural belt and 75 percent of them were from the Jat Sikh community. BJS urban support base was evident, considering that 56 percent of the party MLAs were from Khatri/Arora caste and another 22 percent were from Bania caste, both urban-based. Congress broader support base was evident as 44 percent of its legislators were from Jat Sikh community, which was a larger number than Akali legislators. The party succeeded in getting elected more Sikh candidates than SAD. To compound its problem, SAD right since its inception has remained divided among the factions. Till the rise of Badal clan supremacy post-1997 elections, there was always an internal conflict of endemic nature over strategy and tactics as well as the leadership.

Aware of its limitations, SAD formed a coalition government led by Sardar Gurnam Singh as chief minister in an alliance with BJS and the Communist Party in 1967 and 1969, notwithstanding the fact that BJS regarded 'the Sikhs as part and parcel of the Hindu society' (Brass, 1974, p. 333). SAD also conceded to accept a three-language policy in 1969. While Punjabi became the first compulsory language and medium of instruction in all the government schools, Hindi and English were also recognised as the second and third languages.

Anandpur Sahib resolutions

It was such a sentiment that found expression in the form of the Anandpur Sahib resolutions of 1973 and 1978. The repeated interference by the centre in the affairs of the state, like the dismissal of Parkash Singh Badal led SAD-Janata Party (mainly the former Jana Sangh members) coalition government and the subsequent attempt by the Congress leaders like Giani Zail Singh to encourage factionalism[7] within SAD, vitiated the political climate in the state and gave rise to anti-centre sentiment.[8] Person-cantered leadership of Indira Gandhi as Prime Minister of India led to the centralisation of political power at the centre to the detriment of the states. Regional parties were viewed with suspicion by the Congress central leadership and it was not averse to misuse the constitutional means at its disposal to dislodge the opposition governments in the states. Autonomist/secessionist movement in the 1980s expressed the same sentiment in more strident form. The core of Akali demands relating to the political, economic, and social relationship between the centre and the state was reflected in the Anandpur Sahib resolution adopted by the working committee of the SAD in October 1973. The resolution incorporated seven objectives aimed to establish the 'pre-eminence of the Khalsa through creation of a congenial environment and a political set up' (Singh, 1981, p. 346).

Main demands raised in the Resolutions were as follows: transfer of the federally administered city of Chandigarh to Punjab; the readjustment of the state boundaries to include certain Sikh majority Punjabi-speaking territory, presently outside but contiguous to Punjab; demand for autonomy to all the states of India with the centre retaining jurisdiction only over external affairs, defence, and communications; introduction of land reforms as well as the subsidies and loans for the peasantry as well as the measures to bring about heavy industrialisation in Punjab; the enactment of an all-India gurdwara act to bring all the historic gurdwaras under the control of the SGPC; protection for the Sikh minorities living outside the state; reversal of the new recruitment policy of the centre under which the recruitment quota of Sikhs in the armed forces fell from 20 percent to 2 percent (Singh, 2005, pp. 111–25; Kumar, 2018).

Consequently the working committee of the SAD added two new demands to the Anandpur Sahib resolutions in February 1981 after which a set of 45 demands were submitted to the centre in September in the same year. These included, among others, the halting of reallocation of available waters of riparian Punjab to non-riparian states. Under the federally regulated arrangements, 75 percent of the river waters of Punjab were to be shared by the neighbouring states (Pettigrew, 1995, p. 5).

Rise of militancy

The repeated failures in the negotiations with the central government that began in October 1981 led to the intensification of the second phase of SAD led mass agitation. This ultimately led to the rise of the political forces who were now demanding an independent state. Militancy in Punjab was already simmering in the form of the rise of Jarnail Singh Bhindranwale received further impetus after the military action by the central government to flush out the militants who had taken shelter in the Golden Temple premises. Operation Bluestar was followed by Operation Woodrose, another military action under which the villages were cordoned off to search for hiding militants. These two actions did not go down well with the community, bringing back the haunted memory of the past. The anti-Sikh riots that followed after the assassination of then Prime Minister Indira Gandhi by her Sikh guards in Delhi and other parts of India further alienated the Sikh community. Akali leaders, most of whom were released only in March 1985 after spending months in jail during the post-Operation Bluestar period, made an attempt to save Punjab from the rise of religious fundamentalism and militancy. As a result, Rajiv Gandhi entered in to an accord with the moderate Akali leader Sant Harchand Singh Longowal on 24 July 1985. In the face of stiff opposition from Haryana and the assassination of Longowal shortly after, the accord proved to be a failure. The Rajiv Gandhi government coming under pressure due to eruption of corruption charges and also the fear of losing support in neighbouring Haryana also restricted the manoeuvring capacity of the government to implement the accord (Kumar, 2004a).

The post-Bluestar period witnessed clear ascendance of radical autonomist forces as the moderate forces lost credibility and legitimacy in a surcharged atmosphere. It took some time for moderate Akali leadership to overcome the tumult and trauma of these events. Even after the Longowal-Rajiv Gandhi Accord, traditional party supporters and many leaders shifted loyalty to ultra-radical elements. What also did not help was the fact that the SAD government led by Surjeet Singh Barnala, which had come to power in September 1985 after the state underwent a stint of emergency (October 1983–September 1985), did not last long. Its failure was due to the loss of its credibility as it was unable to get the demands agreed upon by the centre like the transfer of Chandigarh to Punjab by 26 January 1986, despite the announcement to this effect. The backing out of the Congress government meant that the Barnala government was viewed as ineffective in fulfilling the panthic agenda. Coming together of pro-militant organisations in the form of United Akali Dal and the targeted killings by the militants of Hindus further weakened the Barnala government. The entry of the state police in April 1986 on the Golden Temple premises to again flush out the hiding militants saw the desertion of Parkash Singh Badal and Gurcharan Singh Tohra–led factions from the party and the government. Meanwhile, the militant violence escalated. As a result, Punjab witnessed increased level of communal polarisation. The continued efforts to create divisions within the different factions of SAD by the Congress leadership at the centre[9] further weakened the support base of the moderates, leading to the subsequent dismissal of Barnala government in May 1987 on the eve of Haryana assembly elections. Subsequently, the state once again came under non-representative central rule for close to five years.[10]

During this turbulent period, SAD came under the firm control of the radical elements and the elements supportive of militancy and the moderate elements got completely marginalised. The dominance of the radical elements became clear by the victory of the SAD (Mann) in November 1989 Lok Sabha elections. The party won six out of the eight seats it contested, securing 29.19 percent of the votes polled. The party now clearly stood for the right to self-determination under the presidentship of Simranjit Singh Mann that had earlier found expression in the form of Amritsar declaration. The marginalisation of the two moderate factions of Akali Dal led by Badal and Barnala was evident as the two factions put together managed to win only 6.65 percent of the votes polled and could not win a single seat. In 1992 both the Akali Dal factions led by Mann and Badal Parkash Singh boycotted the Lok Sabha and assembly elections that took place one year after the 1991 Lok Sabha elections held in other states.

Revival of electoral politics

It was only in the mid-1990s that 'normal' politics appeared to be making a comeback. The process started with holding of assembly elections in 1992 despite the threats of the militants and the call for election boycott by Akalis. Electoral turnout as a result was drastically low. However, the Congress government led by Beant Singh credited itself by flushing out militancy from the state with the help of Punjab police and the local mass support. The Congress government at the centre led by Narsimha Rao gave free hand to the state government. Even after the assassination of Beant Singh in 1995 on 31 August, militancy could not make a comeback as masses had completely turned against them. The 1997 assembly elections as a result were peaceful/ normal elections that took place after a long period. Significantly, emergence of a sharp and shrill politics of Hindutva in the 1990s did not make the state to go back to its turbulent ethnic past. The same can be said about SAD as the moderate leadership of Badal ensured that the radical elements were marginalised.

Apart from the moderating influence of Parkash Singh leadership over the party, it was the electoral compulsions of the party also that shaped the politics of the SAD. The party being a constituent of NDA led by the BJP and sharing the power at the centre helped in moving SAD towards seeking cooperation from the centre. The dire financial situation of the state post-militancy also compelled the party to keep away its adversarial approach towards the centre.

SAD (united) came in to existence in 1994 uniting as many as six Akali factions comprising of radical elements the name of panthic unity primarily due to the efforts of Bhai Manjit Singh, the then acting Jathedar of Akal Takht. However, the SAD (Badal) retained its separate existence under the leadership of Parkash Singh Badal. Gradually, however, as the urge for peace and Hindu-Sikh unity became strong, SAD (Badal) emerged as the dominant faction being able to integrate almost all the constituents of United Akali Dal in the course of time with the notable exception of SAD (Mann).

Typical of its fractious history, SAD led by Badal was split again on the eve of the 1999 parliamentary elections as Gurcharan Singh Tohra, the long-term president of the SGPC for close to two decades, raised the banner of revolt against Badal with the help of the then Akal Takht Jathedar. The Sarb Hind Shiromani Akali Dal (SHSAD) was formed under the leadership of Tohra on 30 May 1999. It formed an electoral alliance with SAD (Mann), SAD (Panthic), and SAD (Democratic). The different factions fought both the Lok Sabha and the assembly elections separately in 1999 and 2002, respectively, contributing to the dismal performance of Akalis in both elections, as would be discussed in the following part of the report. Congress, which had a poor run in 1996, 1998 Lok Sabha, and 1997 Assembly elections, was able to make electoral gains because of division in Akali vote.

The ascendancy of SAD (Badal) over other Akali Dal factions by the end of the millennium can be explained in terms of Badal family's control over both SGPC and the Akal Takht, the highest temporal and religious seats of the Sikh community. Besides giving legitimacy and religious sanction, the SGPC has always been the major source of funding for the party as donations keep coming to gurdwaras under its control. In the pre-Badal era, both the SGPC and Akal Takht had enjoyed a certain degree of autonomy in relation to the SAD.

Why have Akalis constantly been looking to stitch together an electoral alliance with a non-Congress parties whether BSP or BJP? And why has Congress, of late, not shown much inclination to have an alliance with other parties?[11] Also, what has led the SAD of late to 'appeal to the Hindus in order to broaden its electoral base or has had to seek electoral alliance with other political parties' (Deol, 2000, p. 100)? As discussed earlier, it has been the realisation on the part of the Akalis fairly early that it would be difficult to come to power on its own even in a Punjabi-speaking state with nearly 54 percent Sikh and 44 percent Hindu (Kapur, 1986, p. 216). This despite the fact that a 'united' Akali Dal could pose a formidable challenge to the Congress, as has been visible in the last decade. Instead of ensuring unity within the party, Akali leadership, for major part of its existence, kept on looking for alliances with other parties, i.e. first with the BSP and then with the BJP, while pursuing its agenda of ousting the Congress from power.

Arguably, electoral alliance with the Bharatiya Jan Sangh and then with the BJP has benefitted the SAD more than it has helped the BJP. Alliance has not only allowed the SAD to have a higher number of seats to contest in the coalition but also plays a decisive role in allotting the seats in the state in accordance with the party's strength. Thus, not only the SAD has been able to give higher representation to the Sikhs in terms of tickets distribution but also in the coalition government whenever the alliance comes to power. SAD leadership has also managed to allot to itself the maximum number of seats under coalitional arrangement in the politically most significant Malwa region where the party has been on stronger ground. The alliance has also allowed the SAD to register its electoral presence in the urban and semi-urban areas of the state and even the party since the 2007 assembly elections has started giving tickets to the Hindus in the urban constituencies, many of them actually winning on Akali tickets. Most of the Hindu candidates fielded by SAD belong to the urban trading castes, traditionally the supporters of the BJP. Moreover, the BJP being the coalition making party at the centre has also helped Akalis to not only share power at the centre in case NDA comes to power but also to expect a transfer of resources from the centre to the cash-strapped economy of the state reeling under an agrarian crisis.

BJP on the other hand has not gained much from its electoral alliance with SAD in terms of spreading its support base across the regions and social groups. The party has of late been viewed as an ineffective partner in the coalition government and is thus unable to benefit its traditional urban social constituency. SAD, when heading the coalition governments in the past, has claimed credit for all governmental initiatives in urban Punjab. The BJP has also been constrained to underplay its ideological thrust, thus further alienating its core support base whereas SAD has until now been able to retain its core rural panthic support base despite advocating an inclusive political and economic agenda. What has gone in favour of the BJP is the fact that such a coalitional arrangement with the SAD acted as a precursor of similar state-level pacts with other state parties like Janata Dal (S), Biju Janata Dal, Shiv Sena, Trinamool Congress, and Asom Gana Parishad. These alliances helped BJP, a north India party confined to Hindi-speaking states till the 1980s, to make its presence and gradually strengthen its organisational base in these states with such success that, now after two decades, the party has emerged as a winnable party on its own in states like Karnataka, Assam, and Maharashtra. The 2019 verdict showed the party finally emerging as the main opposition party in West Bengal and Odisha. Punjab has been a notable exception in this regard.

Implications of coalition politics

What has been the long-term impact of the electoral alliances on the politics of the state especially the long-term electoral alliance between the Akali Dal and the BJP, in place since 1997? Arguably, the alliance has forced the two alliance parties to discard radical stances on contentious issues like language or centre-state relations. Lok Sabha and Assembly elections held in Punjab since 1996 have continued to reflect a shift in the electoral politics of the state. The continuation of coalition politics in Punjab has not only witnessed the competitive populism but also on a positive note led to the 'gradual discarding of radical stances by political parties all over the state'. This has been evident in the manifestos of the two parties released in every election since 1997. They invariably promise to help maintaining 'peace, brotherhood, communal harmony, social-economic welfare, all-round development and sustainable and profitable agriculture through diversification'. Notably, the elections held in the last two decades have been fought on the basis of politico-economic issues (development, roads, bridges, octroi, free power and water, traders' demands, water for Punjab farmers, fiscal governance, institutionalised corruption) and not on ethno-religious issues[12] like the Anandpur Sahib resolution, transfer of Chandigarh to Punjab, anti-Sikh riots or fake encounters, as was the case with the elections contested by the SAD. The end of militancy and revival of democratic institutions has witnessed the newfound Akali focus on Punjabi identity than the panthic identity and development and governance issues. The alliance has therefore been viewed as being conducive for ensuring ethnic peace[13] in the state, if not ensuring the development or better governance. SAD in its Moga declaration on 25 February 1996 took the pledge to fight for its demands within the constitutional framework of India. In addition, the shift from an anti-centre stand to cooperative federalism is discernible in all the SAD election manifestos since 1997. In the 2019 elections, SAD contested using the face of Narendra Modi. Taking a cue, Congress, like the state unit of BJP, has also started raising the regional issues like the distribution of river water in favour of Punjab, and state's claim over Chandigarh. In Amarinder Singh, it has got a leader who has got state wide support.

Shifts in the political agenda of the SAD has have effectively brought normalcy into a once troubled state. It resonates with the yearning of the people to break away from 'gurdwara politics' and a hope for lasting peace and prosperity (Jodhka, 2000a). The shift has been possible also due to the emergence of the new breed of Akali leaders who, unlike the old 'Taksali' leaders in the past, have little to do with panthic politics.[14] As the memories of operation Bluestar and anti-Sikh riots fade, and a new generation of youth, which has grown up in the militancy-free peaceful Punjab of the 1990s become the voters as well as the leaders, the secular criteria such as governance and economic policies have taken precedence over the identity politics drawing up on the community and regional aspirations.

Given the ascendance of the BJP as the second 'dominant party' in the 'Modi era', how long this alliance would continue has been a matter of debate especially as the party has not gained from its alliance. Most likely, the BJP would continue to seek a greater number of seats to contest under coalitional arrangement. BJP, however, also realises the critical need to have the support of the regional partners as a coalition-making party. Also there is a lurking danger that any breakup might help the Congress.

Conscious of the possibility of a breakup in future and its natural urge to emerge as single-majority party in the state, there has been a consistent effort on the part of the SAD, especially since the Sukhbir Singh Badal ascendancy to the post of the President of the party, to expand its support base while retaining its core-voting constituency.[15] This has been evident in the way the party of late has been giving tickets to Hindu candidates, mostly in the assembly elections. Hindus have also found place in the party's organisational bodies in the last one and half decades. Realising that Punjab has been rapidly urbanising, the party has, of late, made efforts to present an all-inclusive agenda that has been targeting the urban Punjab and middle classes. Since the 2008 local elections, the SAD has been showing the inclination to fight more and more urban bodies' elections even to the extent of annoying its electoral ally. In addition, the party has sporadically expressed its desire to expand its spatial base beyond Punjab in areas where the Sikhs are in large number like in Haryana, Delhi, and in the Terai area of Uttarakhand.

Notes

1 For a detailed discussion of the agitation for formation of Punjab state, refer Nayar (1968).

2 Except Giani Zail Singh, a Tarkhan Sikh, all the Congress chief ministers in Punjab since 1966 have been Jat Sikhs.

3 'In the case of Punjab the agrarian prosperity of the state was socially located amongst the "rugged" Jat farmers of the state. The discourse of development thus celebrated the Jatness of Sikh farmers and in many ways helped them capture the centre stage of the social and political life in the state' (Jodhka, 1997, p. 279).

4 In the first three assembly elections held in 1952, 1957, and 1962 in Punjab, the party won around 60 percent of the vote.

5 There has never been a colossal loss for either the Congress or the SAD-BJP in terms of votes polled, even when elections have been plebiscitary in nature like the ones held in 1977 (post-emergency) or in 1985 (post-Longowal-Rajiv Gandhi Accord, 1985).

6 Contrary to popular perception, Punjab has always had big cities even during the colonial period.

7 Sharma (1986, p. 635) has observed succinctly that whereas the Congress party in Punjab has been 'defusionist in its inter-party behaviour and accommodationist in intra-party relations', Shiromani Akali Dal has been 'accommodative in inter-party relations, while defusionist in regard to the intra-Akali relations'. Thus, he concludes that 'Congress is the "opposite", or mirror image, of the Akali Dal'.

8 Six factions of SAD, namely SAD (Panthic), SAD (Mann), SAD (Kabul), SAD (Babbar), SAD (Talwandi), and SAD (Manjit Singh), came together on 1 May 1994 following the Amritsar Declaration to form a united Shiromani Akali Dal. However, even then SAD (Badal) did not join it.

9 Viewing regional parties as a threat to the nation's unity and integrity, Indira Gandhi made conscious efforts to weaken them.

10 Assembly election to be held on September 1991 was cancelled by the Election Commission necessitating the extension of central rule, a move supported surprisingly by the CPI (M).

11 The Congress since 2007 assembly elections has been refusing to have an alliance with the Communist Parties in the state. In the 2012 Assembly elections, it refused to enter into alliance with the Punjab Peoples' party, which cost the party. Earlier, when the Left was strong in the state, there was a possibility of Left-SAD alliance given their shared view on centre-state relations in favour of autonomy to the centre and also their common rural support base. However, the SAD refusal to take a clear position against militancy plus the alliance with the Bharatiya Jan Sangh (later BJP) put paid to such a possibility.

12 However, SAD still takes strident position when it comes to panthic issues, claiming to be the sole authority on community-related issues. For instance, the party has been demanding for long the amendment to the SGPC Act, 1925 to prevent Sehajdhari Sikhs from voting in the SGPC elections. Sehajdhari Sikhs, who are mostly Sindhi devotees of Guru Nanak and do not follow the 'five Ks' of the Keshdhari Sikhs, are allowed by the SGPC Act to maintain gurdwaras.

13 The communal harmony theme is reminiscent of the common programme of the SAD-Jan Sangh coalition government way back in 1967 (Singh, 1981, pp. 103–4).

14 Many of the present generation of leaders like Sukhbir Badal coming from political families were sent outside the state during militancy. As a result they were insulated from the contentious politics of the day.

15 SAD government during its tenure (2007–2017) constructed cultural heritage buildings/memorials mainly connected with the Sikh religious figures.

5 Assembly elections in Punjab
1997–2017

After discussing the electoral politics in Punjab from 1952 to 1996 in the preceding section, in this section's focus shifts specifically on Assembly elections held after militancy came to an end. Besides giving empirical details, the overview also aims to present a comparative study of these elections with the objective of highlighting differences in terms of the following: Electoral issues taken up by the parties during the campaign, regions[1] specific trends, alliance formations, and seat adjustments. As a part of this overview, an assessment of electoral verdicts[2] in different elections is also presented, showing and explaining the electoral volatility[3] in the state. The Assembly elections held in 1997 and after have witnessed not only a very high level of electoral participation[4] and contestation but also have marked a distinct shift in terms of electoral agenda cutting across the party lines, as mentioned in the preceding section.

The assembly election held in 1997 was considered the first 'normal' election after militancy was crushed. The election was important in many ways; most important being the fact that all the parties, including SAD, participated in it. In the 1992 Assembly elections, only a breakaway faction of SAD led by Captain Amarinder Singh had fought the elections without any success. All other SAD factions had abstained as dictated by militants who had also threatened the voters to abstain. As a result, the 1992 elections saw a sharp dip in terms of electoral participation with turnout being only 23.92 percent. The boycott benefitted the Congress as the party won as many as 87 seats in the elections whereas the BJP and the BSP fighting alone managed to win nine and six seats, respectively. Despite a question mark hovering over the legitimacy of the election due to boycott and low turnout, the 1992 elections did revive the democratic process after five years of president rule. Revival of the democratic process helped Beant Singh lead the Congress government to combat militancy in active cooperation of the centre. Within a year, the state government was able to hold local bodies' elections, which witnessed massive electoral participation, marking the revival of political activity in the state after long lull.

As mentioned in preceding chapters, the Assembly elections held in 1997 marked the beginning of SAD entering into alliance with BJP. Consequently,

SAD broke its alliance with BSP that had been in place during the 1996 Lok Sabha elections. The 1997 elections took place at a time when political parties, in the wilderness during militancy, were trying to recapture their political relevance and shed their tainted image as being communal parties. During the height of communal frenzy that swept the state during the turbulent period, the parties were viewed as pandering to a particular community so while the SAD was viewed as a Sikh party, Congress was dubbed as a Hindu party in the state and was squarely blamed for Operation Blue Star and anti-Sikh riots in Delhi that followed. It was during the period of militancy that the left parties, i.e. CPI and CPI (M), suffered an irreversible decline in terms of their support base as their party cadres came under attack. In the last three decades, the left forces have had negligible presence, and have been confined to the Malwa region.

Besides marking the return of mainstream politics, the Assembly elections in 1997 also witnessed the comeback of the 'traditional leaders' and Sikh institutions, who had been 'marginalised during the militant era'. This notwithstanding that it was their 'factional struggles and political failures [that] had played a part in exacerbating militancy' (Dyke, 2009, p. 976). Since then the radical elements in favour of reviving the autonomist movement based on religious nationalism, represented by the parties like Dal Khalsa or SAD (Amritsar), have failed to secure any electoral success.[5]

The 1997 election was also important in the sense that it marked a perceptible shift in the political agenda as communal peace and unity replaced the sectarian ethnic agenda that had dominated the politics of the state during the period of Punjabi Suba movement and militancy. The Akali Dal-BJP alliance[6] stitched on the eve of the 1997 elections was a manifestation of this shift which apparently had electorates' support. The very fact that the Akali Dal-BJP alliance got massive electoral support was construed as reflection of people's trust that the alliance would be instrumental in restoring peace and communal harmony in the state. It was this popular urge that was a factor in SAD sharing power with the BJP despite getting a majority on its own.

Assembly elections, 2002

Assembly elections in 2002 happened after the SAD-BJP coalition government had completed five years in power. Punjab, after reeling under militancy for more than a decade in the 1980s and early 1990s, witnessed political stability and peace during the period. It was for the first time that the SAD[7] was able to complete its full term in power, thus negating the popular perception that the SAD as a party, being badly divided among factions and being always in agitation mode, was not capable of governing or giving a stable government.

The change in government was, however, very much in the cards, given the fact that, since the state reorganisation, electorates in Punjab were alternatively voting for the SAD and the Congress in varying permutations and combinations. Also the 1990s was a period marked by a very high level of volatility in India as anti-incumbency was a major electoral factor. Victory for the Congress fighting elections in alliance with the CPI was thus expected. Again, typical of the electoral trend in the state, the margin of the victory of the Congress was narrow. The final tally of 63 seats with 38.2 percent of total votes polled gave the Congress-CPI alliance a small majority of four seats in an assembly of 117 seats. The SAD-BJP managed to win 44 seats with 36.6 percent of the total votes polled. In effect, a less than 2 percent swing of votes would have reversed the electoral outcome. As for the remaining six seats, they went to independent candidates. The Sarb Hind Shiromani Akali Dal (SHSAD)-SAD (Mann)[8] combine forming 'Panthic Morcha', which had 13 members in the outgoing assembly, did not win any seat but polled at 4.4 percent of the vote at the cost of the SAD; as being the supporter of the revival of religious nationalism, they sought the traditional Sikh vote. The other mainstream opposition parties like BSP, the Nationalist Congress Party (NCP), and the Scheduled castes Bahujan Samaj Morcha (DBSM), an ally of the SAD, also drew blanks in terms of both seats and votes, setting the trend for coming years (Kumar and Kumar, 2002).

Compared to the 1997 elections, the electoral verdict in the 2002 elections was a great climb down for SAD-BJP alliance, both in terms of seats and vote percentage. The SAD-BJP alliance lost 44 seats and more than 9 percent of the popular votes polled. In the 1997 elections, the alliance had polled 45.97 percent of the votes and won 93 seats (75 and 18, respectively). The INC-CPI alliance in 1997 elections had won merely 16 seats with the Congress polling 26.38 percent votes, 14 seats, and the CPI polling 2.98 percent votes and winning two seats.[9]

However, if one looked at the difference in terms of the percentage of votes polled by the two allies in 2002 elections, the INC-CPI combine polled only 1.6 percent more votes as compared to the SAD-BJP-DBSM alliance. It was a technical win for the former, if viewed from this angle. This, however, in a way set the trend for the subsequent elections as even a smaller margin of difference in terms of vote has made a difference between electoral win and defeat in the state (Kumar and Kumar, 2002).

How could this disconnect between the seats won and the votes polled by parties be explained in the context of the 2002 election? Besides the simple plurality/first-past-the-post electoral system being a factor, the other possible explanation was the relative performance of the different political parties within two parties' alliances. If one looked at the performance of the Congress-CPI alliance, the Congress while contesting for 106 assembly seats won 62 seats and polled at 36.5 percent of the votes. Its ally, the CPI, however, polled at only 1.7 percent of the votes and won one assembly seats while contesting for ten seats. This explained why, since the 2007 elections, the Congress and the CPI and the CPM have not entered into an electoral alliance since then, as the Congress leadership remains convinced of decline of the left forces.

If one looked at the performance of the SAD-BJP combine separately, SAD, contesting for 90 assembly seats, won 41 seats and its coalition partner

BJP, contesting for 24 seats, managed to win only three seats, polling at 5.7 percent of the votes. The BJP vote share was 7 percent below that of the SAD in the seats it contested. Thus, it was not that the SAD performed too badly, but the alliance suffered mainly due to the poor performance of the BJP. Most of the votes polled by the BJP, it was obvious, could not be converted to winning assembly seats. Another minor ally, the DBSM, lost both the seats it contested, further adding to the woes of the SAD. As many as six SAD rebels won contesting as independents, damaging the party electorally.

Arguably, if SAD had allied with the BSP in this particular election and the two parties would have been able to transfer their votes to each other,[10] then the combine would have got at least four more seats as the BSP was still a political force in the state then. Such an argument gained credence if one refers to the 1996 Lok Sabha elections results when the SAD in alliance with BSP had taken lead in the assembly segments with sizeable Scheduled castes population like Samrala, Kartarpur, Dhuri, Dirba, Lehra, Talwandi Sabo, and Nihalsinghwala, but lost all of them in 1997 Assembly elections when the alliance broke up. The BSP contesting alone could win only one seat despite contesting 67 seats, though it emerged second in as many as nine constituencies. The electoral dividend that alliance with the BSP would have provided to the SAD in this election was obvious, as BSP still seemed a relevant party with its proven record of being able to transfer its core vote (dalits) to its electoral ally.

How could the electoral outcome in 2002 be compared with the 1997 elections, if viewed from electoral regions? Congress had suffered heavily in the Doaba and Majha regions in the 1997 Assembly elections, particularly in the western constituencies of Doaba bordering the Majha region where the militancy had a high presence. Congress had lost all the 24 seats it had contested, whereas SAD had secured victory in all 18 seats it contested in Majha (27 assembly seats). In the Doaba region, also the Congress had succeeded in winning only 5 against 25 seats it contested as against the SAD electoral success in 13 out of 16 seats. In the Malwa region, the SAD won 44 out of 58 seats it contested. Its ally, the BJP, on the other hand, won seven out of eight seats in Majha region, five out of eight in Doaba region, and all six in Malwa region. Now in the 2002 Assembly elections, the Congress-CPI combine gained in all three regions as SAD-BJP alliance suffered from a massive negative swing of the votes (12.3 percent) and a loss of 18 assembly seats. Congress won 17 seats from Majha region and polled at 40.6 percent of votes. SAD-BJP alliance, on the other hand, won only seven assembly seats from Majha and polled 39.1 percent of the votes polled. In Doaba also, SAD-BJP alliance fared badly, winning only nine seats with 35.4 percent of votes as against the 16 seats won by the Congress-CPI alliance with 39.4 percent of the vote. In the Malwa region, the SAD-BJP-DBSM electoral alliance did relatively better by winning 28 seats with 36 percent vote as compared to 30 seats won by the rival INC-CPI combine with 37 percent of the vote. The swing in favour of Congress was the lowest in Malwa compared to other regions.

What can be the possible explanation for the electoral defeat of the SAD-BJP-DBSM alliance in this close electoral contest?[11] Possible explanations to the electoral reversal would include the following: the anti-incumbency factor; the emergence of the radical panthic morcha dividing the traditional panthic vote; the tussle for taking control of Akal Takht among the different factions of SAD; the failure of SAD-BJP regime in implementing the promised special border area programme for the farmers who were dispossessed of their cultivable land due to the fencing of the border and also became potential victims of land mines laid in the area as well as evacuation due to frequent border skirmishes in the constituencies like Ajnala, Raja Sansi, Attari, Valtoha, Patti, Nausherhra Pannuan, Fatehgarh Churian, Dhariwal, Dinanagar, and Narot Mehra; the lack of clean and efficient governance; the production-oriented farming reaching a plateau in a post–Green Revolution Punjab; the reckless pursuit of the policies of economic populism like supplying free electricity and water to the farmers, resulting in erratic supplies and fiscal deficits; the suicides by the cotton farmers in the districts of Muktsar and Faridkot; the Supreme Court decision on the Sutlej-Yamuna Link (SYL) canal directing the Punjab government to complete it within one year; the unprecedented nepotism in the distribution of tickets controlled by Badal family (a new factor then) that resulted in to a 'rebel factor'. Dismal performance of its ally BJP could be attributed to following factors: the delayed decision of the coalition government to abolish octroi, the erratic power situation in the urban area, the pro-rural slant of the coalition government, and the perceived marginal role of the BJP in the alliance. Minor parties like the BSP and the NCP contesting on their own never had a chance except playing the role of spoilers (Kumar and Kumar, 2002).

As for the poor performance of Panthic Morcha representing radical Sikh elements, it could be due to four factors: first, Morcha failed to put up strong candidates in most of the constituencies. Second, Morcha had very limited influence both in terms of the number of constituencies and community primarily due to the religious component[12] in its agenda. Third, there was lot of internal dissension within the Morcha with the leaders like Tohra,[13] Mann, and Baba Sarabjot Singh Bedi (the convener of the Morcha) competing against each other to have an upper hand. Fourth, Morcha suffered due to its failure to tie up with the Bahujan Samaj Party despite an early breakthrough, as the BSP leadership reportedly asked for 80 seats.

What went wrong for the SAD-BJP alliance in these elections? Lokniti post-poll survey seemed to suggest possible answers. First, as high as 60 percent of the respondents interviewed felt that political interference (read Akalis) in the religious matters (Akal Takht, SGPC) had increased and 78 percent of them agreed that it had its effect on the electoral voting. Second, out of 65.5 percent of the respondents who had heard about the suicides of the cotton farmers, 58.8 percent either held the Badal government squarely responsible for it or blamed it along with its ally, the NDA government at the centre. Third, 15.5 percent of the respondents held SAD responsible for promoting nepotism in the distribution of tickets. Fourth, showing the rural-urban divide, populist policies of the SAD-BJP government regarding the free supply of electricity to the farmers seemed not to pay electoral dividend as it was considered unjustified by 37.8 percent of the respondents, mainly urban: 36 percent of the respondents felt that it led to an interrupted supply of electricity. Fifth, the SAD-BJP government came under opposition on the prevalence of corruption as 33.8 percent thought that the situation had worsened during the last five years compared to 23.2 percent who thought it had improved.

Post-poll survey data of the Assembly elections held in 1997 and 2002 were helpful in analysing then emergent trends in Punjab politics. In both surveys, respondents interviewed considered SAD-BJP alliance as best suited to keep peace in the state. Also, both the surveys showed the electorates deciding to keep away from sectarian ethnic politics and determined not to let it revived. Only 12.6 percent of respondents in the 2002 survey were willing either to support completely or partially the methods adopted by the militants, whereas 63.2 percent of the respondents went to the extent of fully or partly justifying the method adopted by the police to curb militancy. In both surveys Congress received fair electoral support of all communities, lagging behind the SAD only among the Jat and Khatri Sikh voters in the 2002 survey. As evidenced by the survey results, the support for Congress among the upper caste Hindus meant erosion of their support for the BJP. Every time the BJP has failed to retain its upper caste urban Hindu constituency, it has meant that SAD has had to win the support of the rural Sikh vote, which has not been possible as 2002 survey data revealed the Congress retaining support among a segment of the non-Jat Sikhs (39.4 percent of those interviewed).

Assembly elections, 2007

Assembly elections held in 2007 witnessed again a close electoral contest between two entrenched parties. Intensity was reflected in a record of 76 percent of electoral participation. The contest witnessed a no-holds-barred media war and public utterances verging on personal slandering. Like the high percentage of voting, the electoral outcome was also along the predictable lines as an anti-incumbency factor came to play a role. The SAD-BJP combine won 68 seats with SAD alone winning 49 seats compared to 41 seats in the 2002 elections and BJP gaining an all-time high of 19 seats compared to a mere three seats in 2002. In a major departure from the past, the SAD headed now by Sukhbir Badal, son of Badal senior, looking to broaden the party's support base gave tickets to as many as seven Hindu candidates (Kumar, 2007).

In a major departure from the last three Assembly elections, Congress this time contested alone. It received unconditional support from the Bahujan Samaj Morcha. Congress put up a decent fight by winning 44 seats as compared to 62 in the 2002 poll. Also, like in the earlier elections, minor parties in the state like CPI, CPM, and the Lok Bhalai party who had entered into an electoral alliance, or the BSP, Bharatiya Jana Shakti Party who had fought alone, could not make any electoral impact. It held true also for the splinter SAD factions who came on a common platform in the name of panthic issues. SAD (Amritsar) led by Simranjit Singh Mann, SAD (1920) led by Ravi Inder Singh, SAD (Longowal) led by Prem Singh Chandumajra and Inder Singh Zira, Majha Akali Dal led by Raghbir Singh, along with the radical organisations like Dal Khalsa and Shiromani Khalsa Panchayat came together on the eve of the elections with the aim of having an effective three-cornered fight against the Congress and SAD-BJP alliance. However, the state continued to witness electoral bipolarity. The number of winning independent candidates came down from 11 to 5 this time. Since then, the number has been declining.

What was exceptional about the 2007 elections was the very different kind of electoral verdicts in three electoral regions of Punjab. In the 1997 and 2002 Assembly elections, the winning party had taken the lead in all the three regions (Kumar, 2002, p. 1385). This time the Congress took a notable lead over the SAD-BJP alliance in Malwa region, traditionally considered the stronghold of the Akalis. In Doaba and Majha, the SAD-BJP combine like in 1997 had the upper hand.

What were the possible factors that affected the electoral verdicts at the regional levels? The success of Congress in Malwa region was largely attributed to the directive of a religious sect called Dera Sacha Sauda to its followers to vote for Congress.[14] Congress also received a good response in this cotton belt as it was credited with the smooth procurement of the food grains and the success of newly introduced BT cotton. Among the factors that went against the Congress in the Majha region of Punjab were the following: lack of development in the border areas, illegal colonisation of the urban peripheries, and the inability of the outgoing government to check the rampant drug addiction among the youth. The SAD-BJP alliance received the support of the farmers in the border region of Gurdaspur, Amritsar, and Firozepur districts as their demand to have easy access to their land for cultivation that falls beyond the fencing besides the resumption of monetary compensation was not accepted by the Congress government. The SAD-BJP alliance not only promised the monetary compensation to the aggrieved farmers but also agreed to give proprietary rights to the farmers who were tilling the government land at a subsidised cost. The alliance also received the support among the sizable Rai Sikh community, mostly borderland farmers on the promise of trying to get them Scheduled caste (SC) status. The candidacy of Navjot Singh Sidhu, a popular figure and powerful orator from the Lok Sabha seat of Amritsar on a BJP ticket, enabled the combine to broaden its support bases in the region. From Doaba region, Congress could win only 3 out of 26 seats contested, whereas the SAD-BJP combine won 20 out of 25 seats contested. In the Jalandhar district, which has a large Scheduled castes population in the rural belt, the combine won nine out of ten seats in a reversal of the outcome in the 2002 elections. Despite the poor performance of BSP, Congress could not take advantage. One reason for the success of the SAD in six reserved constituencies was the attempt by it to draft support among the Scheduled caste Sikhs by including their representatives in the reconstituted party's political affairs committee and also by giving tickets to them this time in large numbers.

What went against the Congress besides the usual anti-incumbency factor in the 2007 election? Among the factors that explained the overall Congress loss, the most decisive was the apparent shift in the urban votes comprising of a sizeable number of Hindus, mostly belonging to upper castes that led to the impressive success of the BJP in the urban/semi-urban constituencies like Jalandhar and Ludhiana. The alienation was attributed to the pro-Jat Sikh image of the Amarinder Singh government and also the attempt to dabble in gurdwara politics, something the Congress had never done so openly. Lacklustre performance of the government led by a chief minister, who remained a remote figure even for his own party men, surrounded by his loyalists that included tainted bureaucrats caused the loss of votes. Governance was also stymied by internal bickering between the groups led by Amarinder Singh and Rajinder Kaur Bhattal. It was only after the debacle in the 2004 Lok Sabha elections that there was some serious attempt to bring forth private investment-induced growth. For the purpose, special economic zones were proposed, most significantly in greater Mohali on the pattern of Chandigarh. The move, however, did not bring benefit as the government was accused of entering into shady business deals with big business houses to the detriment of the farmers whose lands were appropriated for the purpose without paying adequate compensation at a time when real estate prices started climbing up. The government also failed to live up to its 'pro-common man' image in the form of the high-handedness of the police against the agitating unemployed/underpaid teachers, doctors, and farmers. In the media campaign the SAD-BJP effectively used photographs showing police excesses even against women protesters. The failure of the Congress to add to the power generation capacity also made it unpopular among the farmers critically dependent on mechanised irrigation. The non-completion of the projects like Ranjit Sagar Dam was highlighted by the opposition. Underlining their pro-farmer image, Akalis promised to set up 600 megawatts thermal plant at Goindwal Sahib and Shahpur Kandi Project. Wrong decisions regarding the distribution of tickets also cost the Congress as many sitting ministers and MLAs lost their seats.[15] Congress gave tickets to only 32 new faces. Giving tickets to non-performing legislators was to check the dissident activities within the party that had cost it heavily in 2004. However, the internal bickering continued. Rivalry between the state Congress unit head Shamsher Singh Dullo (belonging to the late Beant Singh group) and Captain Amarinder Singh came in the way of the concerted effort of the party's top leadership to retain power in this crucial border state. Jagmeet Singh Brar and Bir Davinder Singh, both then CWC members, were other long-standing crusaders against the captain's leadership (Kumar, 2007).

Despite its defeat, the Congress was able to put up a credible performance. Congress benefited from the effective implementation of the ambitious free health insurance scheme for the poor farmers under the Sanjeevini scheme that benefited 4.70 lakh BPL families. Medical treatment worth Rs 2 lakh was made available to them in about 300 hospitals in the state. The recruitment of 1,200 school teachers without any charge of corruption or favouritism, and the abolition of octroi also helped the Congress as the Akalis when in power had failed on both counts. Three-phase extensive 'vikas yatras' undertaken by Amarinder Singh at the fag-end of his reign that was joined sporadically by senior leaders like Dullo, Bhattal, and Lal Singh also helped. The Congress also tried to take credit for giving the country its first Sikh Prime Minister, which went well in the Sikh majority state. The non-performance of the earlier SAD-BJP government (1997–2002) was also a factor that dissuaded a sizable chunk of voters voting for the alliance. In a significant move, reminiscent of the ongoing federalisation of the party system in India, the state unit of Congress had got the assembly to pass unanimously the Termination of Water Agreement Act, 2004 refusing to proceed with the Sutlej-Yamuna Link (SYL) project, much to the annoyance of the high command. The creation of new districts like Mohali and Fatehgarh Sahib in the name of greater development, administrative efficiency, and the decentralisation of power also helped the Congress as evidenced in its wins in closely contested fights in these constituencies. Verdict was typical of the state electoral trend which never witnessed a massive swing in favour of a particular party in 'normal' elections like this (1985 and 1992 elections that took place under the shadow of militancy could be dubbed as 'abnormal' ones).

What were the factors that were in favour of SAD in this particular election? The most decisive one was the new-found unity within SAD under the leadership of Parkash Singh Badal that showed in the fairly early distribution of tickets without much protest. With the demise of Gurcharan Singh Tohra and Surjit Singh Barnala, Badal, ably assisted by senior Akali leaders like late Captain Kanwaljit Singh and Sukhdev Singh Dhindsa, emerged as the undisputed Akali leader in the same league as Baba Kharak Singh, Master Tara Singh, and Giani Kartar Singh. The projection of Sukhbir Singh Badal as heir apparent during the campaign did not receive flak from the senior Akali leaders primarily due to his organisational hold over the party and also because family members of senior Akali leaders were preferred while distributing the party tickets. Thus in many cases both father and son got the party tickets, turning SAD into a 'family party' (Kumar, 2007).

There was no change, however, in one aspect. Both the Congress and the SAD continued to compete against each other in holding out populist promises like earlier elections, without revealing the programmatic efforts to be taken in the event they came to power. SAD had won the elections in 1997 on the promise of free power and water scheme for the farmers. This time, it promised a public distribution of flour for Rs 4 and pulses for Rs 20 to the people below the poverty line if voted back to power (the party was derisively dubbed as the 'Atta Dal' party). Among other impressive promises made by the SAD-BJP coalition in their manifesto (for the first time in English too) were the following: filing up all the government jobs; health insurance and free electricity for the farmers; shagun scheme for the poor girls; old age pension and pension for the disabled, widows, and dependent children; new industrial policy; streamlining of VAT; block-level 'adarsh' schools; ten medical colleges; training institutes for self-employment; joint ventures with foreign universities; free education for girls up to university level; getting rid of land scams, providing sustainable prices for farmers; creating a separate ministry for NRIs with representative offices in Europe, UK, Canada, and the US to protect their property and business interests in Punjab; single window clearance for NRI investments; an international airport at Ludhiana and an airport in Jalandhar; new urban development policies to regulate the haphazard growth besides giving the colonisers and the builders' freedom to plan their projects; urban development with a human face; additional 5,170 MW of power for Punjab by measures like reviving the Goindwal power plant and Bathinda refinery project to add 1,000 MW; one-time debt settlement scheme and staggered debt transfer plan for indebted farmers; a new scheme of free health insurance cover of Rs 2 lakh for every farmer and landless labourers; grant of cooperative education loans up to Rs 10 lakh at a nominal interest to the children of the marginal farmers; farmland to be acquired only with the consent of the affected farmers who were also to be given 30 percent displacement allowances as settled by the local sarpanch, MLA, and the MP; package to the farmers for the second push to the Green Revolution; and the setting up of youth development and employment generation boards.

It was no surprise that the manifesto of the Congress had a similar populist line: rice and flour at Rs 4 and pulses for Rs 20 for the poorest of poor, free power supply to the farming sector, tube well connections to small and marginal farmers within 12 months, taking landowners as partners on board any major project, continuation of MSP schemes, reforming the cooperative sector, reducing the interest on farm loan to 5 percent, streamlining the private moneylenders, creating three new special economic zones, one each in three regions, abolition of sales tax by 2010, reworking VAT, reduction in the turnover tax on trade to 0.25 percent, and equal distribution of water to all parts of the state (unlike SAD, it however did not mention scrapping section 5 of the Termination of Water Agreement Act, 2004 that stipulated that Haryana and Rajasthan would continue to receive water as per their respective shares). Other promises included providing relief to the manufacturing sector from stamp duty and electricity duty and the waiver of the entertainment tax. It also promised to make Punjab an electricity surplus state by 2012, the prompt implementation of the recommendations of Fifth Pay Commission, a greater thrust on the development of IT and biotechnology-based industries, and a lump sum VAT on the brick kiln owners.

BSP dwindling electoral fortune was another feature of this election. Like in the 2002 elections, this time also the party drew a blank. The dismal performance of the party could again be attributed to the internal divide within the dalit community along the lines of religion and caste, their neglect of the top leadership (read Mayawati) that remained focused on UP, their factionalism, and their refusal to enter into strategic alliances.

The politics of Punjab remained lopsided in terms of gender representation. Only 54 women candidates were in the electoral fray, of whom only seven won, all of them belonging to the political families.

Arguably, the electoral outcome was not a positive vote in favour of the SAD-BJP alliance but rather an indictment of the non-performance compounded by the internal bickering within the Congress. In the absence of credible alternatives, the electorates in Punjab like in the earlier elections were forced to go for change without much expectation.

Assembly elections, 2012

The assembly election held in 2012 was significant for at least two reasons. First, as the first tie in the reorganised state, there was some hope of a shift from the long-established bipolar system in the state as PPP, which was setup by Akali rebel Manpreet Singh Badal, had run a highly visible campaign, very well-attended by the youth. Second, for the first time, an incumbent party was able to remain in power after the election in post-1966 Punjab.

The elections registered largely unexpected results[16] across all the three regions[17] in favour of SAD-BJP combine. The results not only stunned the Congress leadership but also proved the pollsters off-guard both in terms of the margin of the win and defeat but the outcome itself. How to explain the unprecedented win? What were the highlights of this particular election?

First, long-drawn intense campaigning by the parties prepared the ground for high turnout at 79.8 percent (male voters lagging behind the female voters by 1 percent) in an elections that saw an all-time high of 1,078 contestants (418 independents).

Second, the state witnessed many yatras (public marches) on the eve of this election. While Punjab Peoples Party (PPP) led Sanjha Morcha comprising of CPM, CPI,[18] and SAD (Barnala) launched Jago Punjab Yatra, Congress embarked on Punjab Bachao Yatra, the ruling SAD undertook Punjab Vikas Yatra. Third, the emergence of the possibility of a 'third alternative' in the form of PPP with its appeal among the state's youth and urban middle classes enthused these voters explains the record turnout. Fourth, given the close nature of verdicts in the state in terms of voting percentage in the recent past and also the rise of the PPP, Congress and SAD went all out for intense campaigning, especially the SAD, with the intent to capture not only the 'floating voters' but also to hold their ground against possible encroachment in their 'vote bank' by Sanjha Morcha. The media hype and the massive crowd in the rallies of Manpreet Singh Badal alerted the Akali leadership to hit the road almost after Manpreet Badal resigned from the SAD government and party in October 2010 (Kumar, 2012a).

Overall, electoral campaign cutting across the party lines concentrated broadly over the performance (or lack of it) of the ruling SAD-BJP combine at the state level and Congress-led UPA at the centre. As a result, the critical issues, earlier finding space in the manifestos only, like the issues of unemployment, corruption, farmer's suicides, school education, cancer deaths in the cotton belt, massive indebtedness, and the power situation this time dominated the proceedings with the ruling and opposition parties making claims and counter-claims (Kumar, 2012).

To substantiate this point, one could refer to the SAD Manifesto released on the eve of 2012 elections in which the panthic/emotive issues like justice for the 1984 anti-Sikh riots, protecting the river waters, inclusion of Chandigarh- and Punjabi-speaking areas, legal reviews of cases Punjabi filed during the days of militancy figured only in half a page. The same page contained also the resolve of the party to preserve peace and communal harmony in a 'futuristic Punjab' (SAD Election Manifesto, 2012, p. 15). As for the leadership issue, the two 'post-Bluestar' generation leaders and also estranged cousins[19] Sukhbir Badal and Manpreet Badal led the intense long-drawn campaigns, which often looked like fratricidal war.

The election saw the emergence of Sukhbir Badal,[20] the deputy chief minister from the colossal shadow of his father within the party organisation. In his capacity as the party President, Badal junior played not only a decisive role in tickets distribution but also worked out the electoral strategy and led the campaign. Living up to his cultivated image of being an 'astute strategist, decisive and entrepreneurial', he chalked out a constituency-specific campaign and candidate selection. An overview of the SAD manifesto, media campaign (control over cable industry helped), as well as the campaign speeches indicated the continued effort of the 'new leader/heir apparent/inheritor' to broaden the party's social support base among the urban mostly Hindu voters while retaining its core support base of rural Sikhs. Listing 'achievements' like building or planning to build expressways, metros, over-bridges, expressways, international airports, solid waste management, and drinking water projects in the cities of Punjab during the campaign underlined the electoral strategy of the SAD to attract the support of the burgeoning urban voters on its own so that the party would not have to remain perennially dependent on its long-standing ally BJP, a party with traditional urban, upper-caste Hindu support base.[21] The conscious laboured efforts to change the electorates' perception of the image of SAD from being a 'panthic' party of Jat-Sikh to a party for 'Punjab, Punjabi and Punjabiat' was strengthened by the party's well publicised move to give tickets to as many as 11 Hindu candidates out of which 10 actually went on to win their seats, a trend that had started in 2007 itself, as noted previously. As the community and locality wise analysis of the electoral outcome showed, the SAD reaped the benefits and also helped its struggling ally, the BJP.[22] The attempted 'social engineering' to 'manage' a winnable majority did help as the electoral outcomes showed that the SAD-BJP not only won 36 out of 62 Sikh-majority constituencies as compared to

26 seats won by the Congress, but more significantly the combine also managed to win in 13 out of 19 Hindu majority constituencies as compared to only four seats won by the Congress (Kumar, 2012, 2012a).

In terms of locality specific outcomes, the SAD-BJP combine had a head start over the Congress even in the urban constituencies winning 9 out of 17 urban constituencies as compared to Congress winning only in six constituencies. Again, SAD, considered a party of farmers, retained its traditional support base in rural Punjab by winning 42 out of 66 constituencies as compared to Congress winning only 23 seats.

PPP-led Sanjha Morcha could not do well electorally. The lack of winnability factor went against the PPP, as voters probably did not think that Morcha could defeat the two entrenched parties and so they did not want to waste their vote. Lack of funds and organisation were major impediments for PPP.[23] Manpreet Badal, four times MLA from Gidderbaha and finance minister in Badal government, helped the SAD as anti-Akali votes got split, hurting the Congress. Manpreet Badal had run a long-drawn-out campaign covering every nook and corner of Punjab with an ample dose of symbolism.[24] However, despite his clean image and popularity, he could not succeed against highly resourceful 'election management' of Sukhbir Badal.[25]

Badal senior and Captain Amarinder Singh,[26] the two ageing chief ministerial candidates for their respective parties, promoted 'family politics' by trying to promote their own family members.[27] While Badal Senior allowed Sukhbir Badal to distribute tickets and pack the state cabinet by his close relatives, Congress leaders were not far behind.[28] Congress leaders overdid it this time while cornering tickets for their relatives and cronies with the party facing the 'rebel factor', which was consequently a huge factor in causing the party defeat.[29] Captain, like other top leaders of the party, i.e. Rajinder Kaur Bhattal and Jagmeet Singh Brar to name a few, could not absolve himself from the responsibility as his son unsuccessfully contested. As the anointed chief strategist and tallest leader of the party in the state for more than a decade before 2012 electoral debacle, Captain was viewed as 'inaccessible' to the party cadres and was also unable to rise above the factional politics. This showed in his inability in tackling the rebel factor, which cost the party dearly. In as many as in 14 constituencies, the margin between victory and defeat was very narrow.[30] Captain when in power had also failed to provide an effective and clean government; a fact harped on by the Akalis during the elections while responding to the similar charges of corruption and non-performance against them.[31] The party campaign showed signs of complacency, probably having too much faith in the electoral pattern of the state. Congress was the last party to announce the names of the party candidates (and did so in instalments) and delayed releasing the party manifesto until well after the dates of the elections were announced, thus giving a head start to the SAD-BJP combine in the run-up to the elections.

The lopsided nature of state polity was illustrated in the way Dera episode was played out during the campaign. After Dera Sacha Sauda opened support, which played an important role in Congress winning in Malwa region in 2007 elections, this time Deras reportedly played again a significant role in influencing the electoral choice of their followers, most of whom belonged to the socially and economically marginal groups. As mentioned in the first section, the parties' leadership took recourse to the 'softer' option of cultivating the Deras to 'deliver' the marginal groups votes without undertaking any substantive efforts to democratise the social base of the power structure. The top party leaders in the state like Amarinder Singh, Rajinder Kaur Bhattal, and Manpreet Badal followed by hundreds of the candidates in the fray made rounds of the influential Deras. Even some Akali candidates defying the SGPC directive sought the blessings of the Deras as the panthic party failed to issue a clear-cut directive in this regard.[32] It is this flirting with Dera Sacha Sauda that would cost SAD heavily in 2017 elections (Kumar, 2014b).

How did SAD manage to dent in the traditional support base of Congress among the rural poor? It had much to do with the massive direct transfer of public resources to the rural poor in the form of Atta-Dal, Shagun (monetary help for girls' marriage), and Mai-Bhago Vidya scheme (cycles for the girl students)[33] schemes besides sops for the rich farmers like free power to tube wells. The schemes were operational on the ground despite the economic difficulties. Eighty percent of the poor respondents interviewed during CSDS survey had heard about the Atta-Dal scheme and 70 percent admitted to be beneficiaries. Likewise, 85 percent of the farmers interviewed had heard about the free power to tube wells (in existence since 1997) and 68 were accepted to be beneficiaries. Fifty-five percent of the Scheduled castes families interviewed had benefited from free power, whereas 78 percent of the respondents had heard about it, as per the CSDS-NES data.

SAD in its manifesto made some amazingly unrealistic promises even by 'Punjab tradition' like providing free five Marla plots to all the landless poor in the state, free gas connections for all BPL families, the generation of one million jobs in next five years out of which there would be 200,000 jobs in the government sector, and free laptops to all the higher secondary government schools (SAD Election Manifesto, 2012, p. 20, 29). Congress, not to lag behind, also indulged in over-the-top promises making a mockery of the sanctity of manifestos. The problem with the Congress was that the electorates posed more belief in the Akali Dal indulgence in fiscal profligacy, which besides the popular image was also due to the Congress highlighting the precarious state of state's economy and the need to introduce urgent reformist measures. Congress' belated attempt to remind the rural/urban poor about the welfare and developmental schemes being funded by the Centre and not by the 'bankrupt' government did not cut much ice with the electorates. Out of the 1,147 respondents interviewed, only 31 percent were not satisfied with the performance of the state government, whereas 57.1 percent were either very satisfied or somewhat satisfied. Among the caste/community, Jat Sikhs reported the highest level of satisfaction with the SAD-BJP government underlining the fact that the SAD in this election managed to retain its traditional support base.

What about the much talked paradigmatic shift in the electoral agenda in the state?[34] Identity issues were not raked up during the campaign but the campaign and the positioning of the contending parties left much to be desired. In a state with 'missing girl children' and facing environmental disaster due to the reckless use of mechanised irrigation and fertilisers, neither the Congress nor the SAD during their campaign focused on the issue of female feticide, continuing loss of green cover, unplanned urban growth by land mafia, or polluting rivers and ground water. SAD, which had way back undertaken a long-term initiative called 'Nanhi Chhan' (the little shade) to save the girl child from feticide and also created awareness about environment, seemed to be unwilling to take it forward. The patriarchal character of political culture reflected in the paltry presence of the women as party candidates. Even over the drug menace that by then was visibly threatening to destroy an entire generation of youth, parties failed to come out with a clear-cut roadmap to curb drug peddling in the state except by suggesting organising sports events or building stadiums to keep youth away from drugs. And then, while the convergence of the electoral agenda towards 'developental- ism' was most welcome even if at the rhetoric level given the turbulent history of the borderland state, the uneasiness about the 'personalised' mode of pol- itics which encourages collusion between the state and political institutions for nefarious purposes ('vendetta') at the local level remained.[35]

Assembly elections, 2017

An analysis of the Assembly elections held in 2017 would involve looking for the commonalities and exceptionality that were visible in this particular election and asking whether it was an unusual election or a routine 'normal' one. Also, such an analysis would involve other important questions having longer implications (Kumar, Mahajan, and Kaur, 2018).

Would the entry of AAP after its unexpected success in 2014 Lok Sabha election lead to a long-term shift towards triangular electoral system in the state? Would 2017 elections indicate a long-term shift in the traditional vot- ing pattern in the state? More specifically, would the debutant AAP con- tinue to be a winnable party in the state or would it simply wither away? Could a prognosis based on this particular electoral verdict be made about the future electoral re-configurations/re-alignments? Did the elections under study offer greater/alternative economic and political choices before the electorates? Questions could also be raised about the inroads social media/ technology seemed to make in this election. Was it just hype or there was substance in the popular understanding of the growing role of the social media/technology during campaigning and did it make an electoral impact in the state?

Arguably, in some ways the 2017 Assembly election was just another elec- tion for the state as it exhibited many long-established trends specific to the state. First, the elections witnessed continued presence and importance of the three historical-cultural-geographical regions, long turned into distinct electoral regions. Second, electoral campaigns were about issues related to the development and governance—not the ethnic issues. Secular issues like governance and development figured prominently during the campaign as well as manifestos of the SAD-BJP and the Congress, even though not many details/road maps were presented. The continued decline of the ethnic/radical mode of politics was evident in the fact that the parties like SAD (Amritsar) and Dal Khalsa did not even seem to figure into it. Third, like the earlier elections, the 2017 elections also witnessed a very high level of electoral participation at 75 percent, higher than the national average. Also, like in preceding elections, the participation of the women was also exceptionally high, almost comparable to male participation. Also, the political assertion of the sizeable Scheduled castes population of the state either in the form of BSP performance or at least emergence of a Scheduled castes leader remained absent. Fourth, competitive populism/patronage based on clientelistic rather than programmatic politics continued unabated with all the parties making promises, which was difficult to fulfil (Kumar, Mahajan, and Kaur, 2018).

Significantly, however, there were few important deviations too from the past, turning the 2017 elections into an 'unusual' election. First, the results marked the end of the long-standing bipolar electoral system even if temporarily with the emergence of AAP as the principal opposition party, leaving behind the SAD. This election provided the voters with a credible third alternative.

AAP's remarkable electoral journey in the state commenced with the 2014 Lok Sabha elections. AAP's success defied the conventional electoral wisdom, as it was a new party pitted against two well-entrenched parties, having a history of a hundred years or so in a state where religion and caste have played crucial roles in varying manner in determining the electoral outcomes in successive elections and the Congress and the SAD being past masters of the game. AAP success was also remarkable, as any party in order to do well electorally needs to have a strong organisational structure, an ideology/definitive positioning on the social and the economic issues and a core social constituency often based on a primordial identity. Also, a winnable party needs a set of credible state-level leadership. AAP was handicapped on all these counts and was considered as being prone to more electoral failures than successes.

This partly explains why the AAP success in 2014 election in Punjab was viewed as an aberration, more so as the party soon after its impressive debut seemed poised for free-fall due to dissidence/expulsion/allegation against the state party unit leaders sent from Delhi. However, by winning 20 seats and polling 23.7 percent of the votes in 2017 elections, the party emerged in the role of a game-changer by effecting a transition from the bipolar to triangular electoral system.

It was noted earlier that the SAD has always set the political agenda of Punjabi Suba after 1966, whether in power or not. However, AAP in this election at least emerged as the clear game changer by setting the agenda, identifying and defining the two electoral issues, i.e. widespread corruption and drugs, that dominated the campaign. The party also issued separate manifestos targeting distinct social and economic categories trying to turn them into voting communities based on their class interest rather than caste or religion. It also facilitated direct involvement of the party's volunteers in selecting the party's candidates, insisting on a thorough background check on the candidates seeking tickets. Interestingly, two older parties adopted many components of the AAP manifestos/campaign strategies, especially the Congress whose chief campaigner and the chief ministerial candidate Captain Amarinder Singh launched Halqe Wich Captain, moving from one part to another, having direct interaction. Both the SAD and the Congress remained active on the social media front as the state witnessed an unprecedented parallel campaign on social media, unleashed by AAP volunteers.

The 2017 elections also witnessed another new development in the electoral politics of the state in the form of the emergence of a new voting community, namely the youth of the state, though it was more visible during the campaign than in terms of actual voting. As per the data provided by the office of the Chief State Electoral Officer of Punjab, at the time of election, 53 percent of eligible voters fell in the age group of 18–39. More crucially, out of 1, 99, 63, 346 eligible voters in all, 9, 68,128 fell in the age group of 18–19. Due to the popular perception that a large chunk of youth had voted for AAP in 2014 elections, the older parties at this time took note of the youth, treating them for the first time as a distinct voting category. Evidence of this was in their manifestos as well as their campaign strategies. Congress Manifesto promised at least one job to every household (55 lakh) in the state, a stipend of Rs 2,500 for the jobless, an end to the drug menace within four weeks of coming to power, and one-lakh taxis/commercial vehicles every year for unemployed youth. BJP and SAD in their separate but uncannily similar manifestos also promised 10 lakh jobs over five years, free laptops, and free higher education for girls. To address the youth aversion for corruption, SAD even pledged to appoint a Lokayukta if voted to the power for the third time. AAP, however, managed to trump its rivals by coming out with a separate youth manifesto. The party made elaborate promises to the youth like 25 lakh new jobs in five years, entrepreneurial/skill centres, end to favouritism in public employment, improved schooling, special laws to give life terms for drug traffickers, end to corruption/crony capitalism, and the appointment of a Jan Lokpal on Delhi model. Then, again taking a leaf out of the AAP book, the campaigns of different parties also showed a sense of urgency to connect to the youth. While all the three parties promised better internet connectivity, the Congress led by promising 50 lakh smart phones to youth who participated in its 'Captain Smart Connect' campaign. Captain also launched 'Coffee (and not Punjabi Lassi) with Captain' mainly to connect with the urban youth in small gatherings across the state. The Congress high command's policy of 'one family one ticket' was also aimed at the youth who abhor nepotism and also to negate the charge of nepotism against it by AAP. Sukhbir Badal, the SAD president had launched 'Youth for Punjab' campaign to make the youth aware of the development work done by the government in the past decade by the SAD-BJP government. All these parties used the social media extensively to connect to the tech-savvy youth, but here too the AAP had the edge during the 2017 campaign (Kumar, Mahajan, and Kaur, 2017).

In terms of leadership also, the election was unusual as for the first time in Punjab electoral history, Arvind Kejriwal, a non-Punjabi-speaking Hindu from the neighbouring state of Haryana with which the state has had a running feud linked to water and territory issues, emerged as the sole face of the AAP campaign in the state and seemed to cause a scare to stalwarts like Parkash Singh Badal and Amarinder Singh, both having a political inning for more than 50 years and enjoying a state-wide support base across the three electoral regions of the state. Significantly, in the run-up to the elections the message was given by the AAP leadership including Manish Sisodia, the Delhi Deputy Chief Minister, that in case of the party's victory, the state government was going to act at the behest of Kejriwal. The Kejriwal factor obviously did not work ultimately in favour of the AAP, but it was quite unprecedented in the state's electoral history.

The 2017 elections also witnessed a significant shift in the traditional social support base of the parties, especially in case of the SAD, a panthic party. SAD always managed to gain decent support of its core social constituency of rural voters, especially the Jat Sikh landed peasantry even when it did not do well in the election, going by the CSDS post-poll data. The party faced this time an alienated rural constituency on account of repeated crop failures, followed by inadequate and erratic compensation to aggrieved farmers, spurious pesticides being distributed by the government, a flawed crop procurement process adopted by government agencies, farmers' suicides, and the issue of minimum support price. Most significantly, the inability of the SAD-BJP coalition government to capture the culprits responsible for the repeated desecration of holy Guru Granth Sahib (Adi Granth) in different parts of the state in the months preceding the elections alienated the party's panthic voting constituency. SAD desperate attempt to enlist Dera Sacha Sauda support just before the election was another development that annoyed the rural Sikh constituency of SAD to no end as the Dera chief was facing serious criminal charges for which he was ultimately convicted: way back in 2007, he was accused of impersonating himself like the revered tenth Sikh Guru Gobind Singh. That a self-proclaimed 'panthic party' leadership would be seeking the support of supposedly 'anti-Sikh' institution showed conclusively the transition of the party into a 'mainstream' electoral party seeking to maximise its vote, especially that of the lower classes that flock to the Deras (Kumar, 2014b).

Let us discuss the 2017 electoral verdicts in terms of votes polled and seats won while focusing mainly on the relevant parties namely the SAD (and BJP), the Congress and the AAP. The verdict shows that the Congress made a significant advance in all the three regions of the state—Majha, Malwa, and Doaba with 38.50 percent vote share (for region-wise electoral performance in 2012 and 2017 elections, refer to Table 5.1). However the SAD also received 25.24 percent votes, though the SAD-BJP combine lost 11.28 percentage points in its vote share from 2012, while the Congress just retained its vote share. The 2017 elections saw a drastic reduction in the vote share of independent candidates, in the 2012 elections they had managed to win only three seats with the vote share of 6.75 percent. Out of these three winning candidates, two candidates were the rebel candidates belonging to the SAD. But in 2017 elections, independents secured a 2.33 percent vote share without winning any seat. Except the Congress, SAD, BJP, and the AAP, other parties in the fray could not even secure 2 percent of the vote polled, leading to the emergence of a triangular electoral system. BSP just managed to secure 1.59 percent of the vote share. Congress improved in terms of winning seats in all the three regions Doaba, Majha, and Malwa as compared to the 2012 elections. But SAD had its worst performance in all three regions. The BJP and independent candidates were big losers in the elections. If we compare 2012 and 2017 election results, Congress added 36 seats to its tally of 46 seats in the 2012 Assembly elections out of the 117 seats it contested. SAD and its partner BJP won only 18 seats, 50 seats less than 2012 elections out of 117 seats it contested. Congress lost 14 seats by narrow margins in 2012 elections, whereas in 2017 its tally of seats lost by narrow margin got reduced to only four seats. This showed the sincere efforts of the Congress leadership to deal with the rebel factor and credit must go to Captain Amarinder Singh as he introduced one family one vote system that helped in keeping dissidence in check. AAP also lost four seats by narrow margin. This time total seats also reduced in terms of fewer margins in 2012 when it was 17, in 2017 it got reduced to 11. As mentioned previously, the most significant factor of the 2017 elections was the presence of the third alternative face of the AAP for the voters of Punjab. The party secured a 23.72 percent vote share by adding 20 seats to its tally; it retained its 24 percent vote share of 2014 elections when it was not considered a winnable party.

How to explain SAD's dismal performance with the party recording lowest number of seats since the reorganisation of the state? Winning for the third consecutive time was never going to be easy for the SAD-BJP combine in a state where only once in 2012 elections the incumbent party was able to retain power. However, to lose so badly after all these years as the percentage of votes polled in favour of SAD in 2017 elections also got considerably reduced in 2017 needs to be explained further. The CSDS-NES survey data shows that the party lost significantly the support of its core social constituency (Jat Sikh peasantry). Besides the reasons stated earlier, the foremost reason for the Akali overall loss of vote was due to the inability of the party regime to stem the economic slide in the post–Green Revolution period as besides the agricultural sector, even the once famed manufacturing sector of the state (refer sports goods/woollen/hosiery/cycle/tractor/small machine parts, among others) suffered decline. On the front of governance also, the SAD-BJP regime failed badly with rampant crime and corruption involving

Table 5.1 Performance of Political Parties from 1967 Onward: Assembly Elections in Punjab

Year of Assembly Election	Party Name BJP		BSP		CPI		CPM		INC		SAD		IND	
	Seats Won	Votes Polled	Seats Won	Votes Polled	Seats Won	Votes Polled	Seats Won	Votes Polled	Seats Won	Votes Polled	Seats Won	Votes Polled	Seats Won	Votes Polled
1967	09 (Jan Sangh)	9.36%	–	–	05	4.85%	03	3.27%	48	37.70%	24 (AD Sant) 02 (AD Master)	20.49% 4.4%	09	16.06%
1969	08	9.01%	–	–	04	4.84%	02	3.07%	38	39.18%	43	29.36%	04	8.89%
1972	00	4.96%	–	–	10	6.83%	01	2.93%	66	42.84%	24	27.65%	03	12.72%
1977	Janata Party-25	14.93%	–	–	07	6.50%	08	3.50%	17	33.58%	58	31.43%	02	9.92%
1980	BJP-01	6.43%	–	–	09	6.49%	05	4.39%	63	45.19%	37	26.69%	02	6.52%
1985	06	5%	–	–	01	4.3%	00	1.9%	32	37.9%	73 (AD Longowal)	38.6%	5	11.9%
1992	06	16.68%	09	16.20%	04	3.48%	01	2.73%	87	43.89%	03 (AD Kabul)	5.83%	05	–
1997	18	8.33%	1	7.48%	2	2.98%			14	26.59%	75 (AD Badal)	37.64%	6	10.87%
2002	3	5.67%	0	5.69%	2	2.15%	–	–	62	35.81%	41	31.08%	9	11.27%
2007	19	8.28%	0	4.13%	0	0.76%	–	–	44	40.90%	48	37.09%	5	6.82%
2012	12	7.18%	0	4.29%	0	0.82%	–	–	46	40.9%	56	34.73%	3	6.75%
2017	03	5.4%	00	1.5%	00	0.2%	AAP+ 22	24.9%	77	38.5.%	15	25.2%	00	2.1%

Note: from 1967 to 1972 total Assembly seats were 104, and from 1977 onward it was 117. From 1967 to 1977 election there was the Jan Sangh party. AAP was formed only before 2014 Lok Sabha Elections. AAP+ includes its alliance party LIP for 2017 elections.

Source: CSDS Data Unit.

the politicians from the ruling dispensation in league with the heavily compromised/politicised police. Punjab in the last decade witnessed an unprecedented level of mafia-style corruption, whether it was related to sand, transport, cable, or liquor—all of them flourished under the politician-bureaucracy nexus. Even the Badal family's vast business concerns from transport to cable to hospitality came under the opposition parties' scrutiny.

What, however, damaged the SAD credibility the most for the voters was the government's inability to check the rampant drug trade in the state, which ruined thousands of the state's youth. Given the high cost of the synthetic drugs, which became easily available all over Punjab, it was basically only the youth from the landed rich peasantry class that could afford it and, as mentioned previously, land belongs mostly to the Jat Sikh peasantry, the traditional voters of the SAD. In fact, despite all the denials and blaming the BSF to check the smuggling from across the border and also carrying out arrests, the Akali leadership could not shrug off the taint. To a query related to drug menace, a staggering 58.7 percent of the respondents interviewed in the CSDS-NES survey contended that the SAD-led coalition government failed in curbing the drug menace. Respondents at that time showed their strong faith in the Congress party as maximum a 30.8 percent of respondents believed that Congress was the best bet to control the drug menace. People were also not impressed with the overall performance of the coalition government. It was revealed by the respondents' answer. When asked whether the SAD-BJP government in Punjab was to be given another chance to be in power, 61.7 percent of respondents answered in the negative. The SAD Jat Sikh leadership was thus blamed to ruin its 'own children' in its greed; as aforesaid, given the high cost of synthetic drugs, only the children of landed peasantry, mostly Jats, could afford to purchase them. In fact, despite all the denials of being complicit in the drug trade and blaming the BSF to check the smuggling from across the border and also carrying out arrests, the Akali leadership could not shrug off the taint.

The electoral setback to the SAD was to be viewed also in the context of the long-term factors that seem to have harmed the party. Notwithstanding its electoral victories, post-1997 Punjab has witnessed the rise of person-centric leadership within the SAD as Badal senior and his close relatives have exercised control over both party and government, while SGPC and Akal Takht autonomy have been badly eroded. Moral authority of Akal Takht over the Sikh community has been badly damaged and both institutions are popularly perceived as instruments of SAD leadership for settling scores with political opponents.

The SAD defeat in 2017 election was also due to the dismal performance of BJP, its long-term ally. BJP contested in 23 assembly seats, allotted to it by the SAD leadership since 1997. The BJP gains and losses in terms of seats or votes in the recent elections has been both attributed to its alliance with the SAD rather than the party's own performance as it has never been able to do well when the SAD has fared badly. Party seemed unable to benefit from its traditional urban social constituency of trading and business groups, who view the party as ineffective in defending their economic interests. The BJP state unit, moreover, unlike in the rest of India has been forced to underplay its Hindutva card due to coalitional constraint. Then, there have been consistent SAD efforts to expand its support base, especially since Sukhbir Singh Badal's ascendancy as the president of the party. As the 2017 results showed, the alliance no longer seemed mutually complementary and therefore electorally beneficial as it was at the time of its inception.[36]

The Congress victory, which seemed to give a lifeline to the party that was on a losing streak across India since its 2014 Lok Sabha debacle, could not be attributed only to the negative vote. There were many positive factors. A very important factor that went in the party's favour was its ability to retain its decent support base both among the Hindu and Sikh electorates, cutting across castes and sub-regions. Another factor that went in favour of the Congress was the chief ministerial candidacy of Captain Amarinder Singh who with his more than five decades of public life and state-wide support base was able to mobilise people's support. What also helped was the reputation of Amarinder Singh being a strong leader who could stand up before the centre for the state's interests, evident in his government's unequivocal stand on the SYL issue in 2004.[37]

Captain's personal popularity was evident in the CSDS post-poll survey. To a question about preference for the next chief minister for the state, a maximum of 29 percent of the respondents voted for Captain whereas 20 percent voted for incumbent Chief Minister Parkash Singh Badal. Arvind Kejriwal, the face of the AAP campaign in the state was the choice of only 6 percent of the respondents, showing clearly that people wanted a Punjabi as chief minister. In response to another query about party best suitable for bringing development to Punjab, 32.6 percent respondents gave their preference for the Congress. SAD was recommended by 23.3 percent; 20.1 percent voted for AAP, whereas BJP got the support of only 3 percent of the respondents.[38] The Congress win may be viewed also as the preference shown by the electorates to settle for continuity and change as while the Congress win allowed them to get rid of corrupted SAD-BJP regime, it also ensured continuity. AAP win would have an element of uncertainty, particularly due to its proximity to Canada-based diaspora.

The most significant development of 2017 elections was the emergence of a third party AAP in the political scene of Punjab. AAP contested for 112 seats and won only 20 seats, but it was successful in fetching 23.7% of the total votes polled (preceded by 24 percent in 2014 Lok Sabha elections), which was really remarkable for the debutant party. The party retaining its support base was significant given the high level of internal dissension within the party. At the same time, there was also increasing realisation about the premature death of the promise of an 'alternative politics' reminiscent of the Anna Hazare–led 'India against corruption movement' (IAC).

As for the dismal prognosis about the future of the party, it can be argued that electoral defeats of the AAP in by-elections held in the last three years, even if bad ones and in succession, are never sufficient causes for the destruction of a party, even if it is a nascent party like the AAP. In any case, the pessimism about the long-term electoral fate of the AAP has always been there to the extent that each one of its few electoral successes, whether in Punjab or in Delhi, has been considered aberrations and for good reasons, as the party still does not have established leadership and also lacks in terms of organisational strength. In the recent years the party has got split and even the remaining leaders keep fighting. So electorally prognosis remains not as good. This is because the party on the ground does not seem to be in self-correction mode.

AAP stood apart from other parties for its conscious attempt to reach out to larger electorates cutting across long-established patterns of partisan alignment/existing social cleavages in the state. The party left its imprint on the politics of the state by raising the issue of drugs, farmers' suicides, corruption, dynastic politics, nepotism, and rampant misuse of public money under the VIP culture in the state. The party succeeded in making corruption in high places as well as the spread of the drug menace the major electoral issues during the campaign. Despite its limited electoral success, AAP's entry rearranged the arena, changed the contest and the electoral strategies in the state.

As per CSDS post-poll survey, to the question, which party raised most important issues, 20.9 percent of the respondents said that AAP had raised the most important issues. The rival parties were forced to take counter-strategic measures to contain the AAP effect during the campaign itself. The newly found Congress government in its first orders decided to do with red beacon culture and has also emphasised over austerity, unheard of in the political culture of Punjab which has been all pomp and show even when the economy is nose diving.

Taking age as a variable, CSDS post-poll survey data from the 2017 elections showed that the Congress party retained its popularity among all age groups almost equally, including the state youth. On the other hand, SAD and BJP in the 2017 election faced considerable loss in their support base among youth and middle-aged voters. Survey data revealed that SAD suffered a great loss from its traditional support base among Jat Sikhs, Khatri Sikhs, and upper caste Hindus as well. On the other hand, Jat and Scheduled castes Sikhs were the major supporters of the AAP. In gender terms, AAP and Congress were more acceptable among men than women voters interviewed during survey. In caste terms, Congress faced a lack of support from OBC Hindus and Scheduled castes Hindu voters and among OBC Sikhs (Kumar, Mahajan, and Kaur, 2017).

Arguably, the emergence of AAP as the third winnable/relevant party also coincided with the emergence of triangular electoral system as, besides the Congress, SAD (BJP as its junior ally), and AAP, none of the opposition parties, i.e. Left parties, SAD(Amritsar), among others, seemed to have any electoral impact whatsoever. This has been the case for quite some time if one refers to the percentage of the votes polled in the recently held elections for both Lok Sabha and the state Assembly. There can be valid scepticism about the possibility of fulfilment of the AAP ambition to emerge as a 'national third force' considering its inherent structural weaknesses and leadership crisis, but the party has definitely emerged as a credible third force in Punjab. Arguably, the party's recent success seems to have weakened the traditional social cleavages impact in the state though one has to wait for affirmation in the ensuing elections. As for the future of the fledgling party in the state, recent assertion of the state unit of the party under the senior leadership of the state taking cudgels with the Delhi-based leadership for undue interference during the electoral process has been held as the reason for the party's dismal performance. The demands have been raised asking autonomy granted to the state unit vis-à-vis the Delhi leadership is a good omen for the party's future in the state but then the state level leaders have also not been on the same page. The eight-year-old party, while continuing to give the 'issue of corruption a new salience in electoral politics and using that as the basis for political mobilisation' like it has done all along its political career in whole of India wherever it has contested, in a major advancement from the past it also took up the state specific issues, forcing the rival parties to respond (Kumar, Mahajan, and Kaur, 2017).

Notes

1 The fourth delimitation exercise undertaken in 2009 changed the number of assembly constituencies in the three regions. The dominance of Malwa region increased as it now has four additional seats to its tally, two each from Majha and Doaba. There has been a complete dominance of Malwa in state politics having 69 total seats; compared to Doaba having 23 seats and Majha region 25 seats.

2 In post-1966 Punjab, no party or coalition government got re-elected except the SAD-BJP combine in 2012.

3 The volatility of the electoral process in Punjab could be attributed to the interplay of the several determinants of its electoral politics like caste, kinship, region, religion, language, and leadership.

4 Voting percentage in the Assembly elections in the post-1966 reorganised Punjab has been 71.18, 72.27, 68.63, 65.36, 64.33, 67.47, 23.82, 68.73, 62.14, 75.36, and 78.6, 76 respectively in 1967, 1969, 1972, 1977, 1980, 1985, 1992, 1997, 2002, 2007, 2012, and 2017. Boycott by the SAD and threats made by militants resulted in low turnout in 1992 elections.

5 Marginalisation of radical elements in the state is evident in the repeated defeats of Simranjit Singh Mann, once a top Akali leader due to the backing of the militants, most recently in 2014 from Khadoor Sahib Constituency. His last electoral victory was in 1999 from Sangrur Lok Sabha constituency.

6 SAD-BJP alliance took shape after the breakup in the SAD-BSP alliance, formed on the eve of 1996 Lok Sabha elections.

7 Indira Gandhi led Congress government at the centre dismissed the SAD-Janata Party coalition government in 1980 after coming back to power at the centre.

8 Simranjit Singh Mann, one-time President of official SAD during the days of militancy, is heading the SAD (Amritsar) at present.

  9 In 1992 Assembly elections, Congress had received 43.71 percent of the votes polled and had won 87 seats. CPI received 3.64 percent of the votes and won four seats. BJP fighting alone polled 16.60 percent votes and won six seats.

10 The BSP has consistently taken a position that while it can transfer its vote to its alliance partner, even when the other parties in alliance with it have failed to do so in the past. This is one reason that the BSP has been bargaining hard while entering into an electoral alliance.

11 Electronic voting machines were used for the first time in this election in the state.

12 Morcha in its manifesto raised the Anandpur Sahib demands and referred to a 'genocidal pogrom' against the Sikhs in 1984.

13 Tohra played a role in pulling down the SAD government led by Surjit Singh Barnala in 1988 when the government ordered operation Black Thunder to flush out militants from Golden Temple (Darbar Sahib). Tohra later joined hands with Badal in 1996 as SAD celebrated its 75th anniversary. After two years, Tohra floated SHSAD following differences with Badal over the historic tercentenary celebrations of the Khalsa birth of at Anandpur Sahib.

14 Dera Sacha Sauda head Sant Gurmeet Ram Rahim Singh directed supporters to support Congress candidates. Radha Saomi, another influential religious sect, also backed Congress.

15 Besides the state party president, the prominent losers among the Congressmen were outgoing cabinet ministers like Jagmohan Singh Kang, Chaudhary Jagjit Singh, Harnam Das Jauhar, Raghunath Sahay Puri, and Avtar Henry. Prominent Akali losers were Tota Singh, Gurdev Singh Badal, and Bibi Jagir Kaur.

16 The SAD-BJP combine with a lead of less than 2 percent in terms of vote share (it actually suffered from a negative vote swing) got a lead of 22 seats over Congress.

17 In 25 constituencies of Majha region, Congress polled 41.2 percent of votes, registering victories in nine constituencies as compared to the SAD-BJP combine receiving 47.2 percent of votes and winning in 16 constituencies. In 23 constituencies of Doaba region Congress received 37.1 percent of votes polled winning in six seats as compared to SAD getting 41.6 percent of vote share and winning in 16 seats. In the crucial Malwa region, Congress received 40.6 percent of votes polled and won in 31 seats as compared to the SAD-BJP combine, which secured victory in 30 constituencies though having less vote share at 40.3 percent.

18 The CPI and the CPI (M) contested from 14 and 9 seats, respectively. All the CPM candidates lost their deposits. Refer to Singh (2012, pp. 22–3) for an analysis of the decline of the Left parties who in 1997 and 2002 elections had electoral alliance with the Congress.

19 One can refer to the political powerful Thakre family in Maharashtra where Udhav Thakre, the 'inheritor' is pitted against his estranged cousin Raj Thakre, the latter forming his own party Maharashtra Navnirman Sena.

20 Symbolic of the changing times, in the election Manifesto released by SAD in 2012, Sukhbir Badal figured for the first time on the cover page.

21 Among the urban voters especially the upper caste Hindu voters, considered the traditional voters of BJP, the SAD-BJP lost up to 10 and 9 percent of votes, respectively, as compared to 2007 CSDS-NES figures.

22 Despite having ideological differences, SAD-BJP alliance has remained intact because of the following factors: the two parties have complementary social support base, the pattern of sharing of power between the self-anointed representatives of the two communities help in striking a semblance of social balance. The most important factor, however, has been the realisation on the party of the

SAD leadership that the party cannot win power on its own as Congress enjoys a support base also among the Sikh community (Kumar, 2004, p. 1516).

23 SAD not only 'bankrolled party nominees but also generously backed Bahujan Samaj Party candidates and Congress rebels to cut into Congress vote'. 'The MBA Programme for Electoral History', *India Today*, April 9, 2012, p. 42.

24 Challenge put up by Manpreet Badal galvanised the SAD-BJP government to go for corrective measures like e-governance and to ensure that the populist pro-poor schemes delivery.

25 Sukhbir Badal has not been the popular choice as chief minister choice as per successive Lokniti surveys. In 2007, 2009, and 2012 surveys only 1.8, 2, and 5 percent of the respondents, respectively, preferred Badal junior as their chief ministerial candidate as compared to 39, 27, and 38 percent for his father.

26 Congress declared Captain as its CM candidate only weeks before 2012 elections. In 2017, the party high command declared him the campaign in-charge and also CM candidate, after he threatened openly to break the party.

27 It is the kinship/family ties that determine the leadership role in both the Congress and certainly in the SAD.

28 During surveys it has been observed that virtually every Punjab village has been witness to politics being defined in terms of '*Gharebandi*' as the family-based loyalties get prioritised over any other consideration in determining the electoral choices.

29 Amarinder Singh's own brother Malwinder Singh rebelled and joined SAD for a brief period after being denied ticket.

30 There were in all eight constituencies where the candidates getting the second largest number of votes polled were Congress rebels turned independents. SAD-BJP combine won from as many as seven constituencies leaving one for the Congress (Judge, 2012, p. 17). One can infer clearly that Congress paid heavily due to internal dissension that was mainly due to the denial of tickets to the deserving candidates, attributed to factional politics and nepotism (Kunbaparasti).

31 In terms of the electorates' choice as Chief Minister in the CSDS survey, Captain was the choice of 33 percent of the respondents interviewed whereas Badal had an edge over him with 38 percent approval.

32 Besides Dera Sacha Sauda, other influential Dears much in demand among the politicians in the elections were Dera Sachkhand Ballan, Piar Singh Bhaniarawala Dera, and Divya Jyoti Jagriti Sansthan (Kumar, 2014b).

33 Women voters showed distinct preference for the SAD-BJP combine primarily due to the welfare schemes implementation

34 Panthic issues were recognised as the most important election issue by merely 2 percent of the respondents in 2012 survey.

35 Singh (2012, p. 21) attributed the SAD victory to its 'war room politics', which involved employment of 'the weaponry of money, muscle power, intoxicants and the media'.

36 State unit of the BJP was contemplating to go separate way in the wake of 2014 results but after the electoral reversal in Bihar in the 2015 election the high command vetoed it, fearful that the breakup would help the rival Congress and also that the Akalis could then revive the panthic agenda, creating trouble in a sensitive border state.

37 Captain had resigned as a minister from Barnala led SAD government in 1986 after the Punjab police had entered into the Golden Temple (Darbar Sahib). Years before he had resigned from the Congress in 1984 after Operation Blue Star despite his close relations with the Gandhi family. More recently, he resigned from his Lok Sabha in November 2016 after the ruling of the Supreme Court of India on the Sutlej-Yamuna Link (SYL) Canal issue. As chief minister of the state, he had got the

Punjab Termination of Water Agreement Act passed unanimously by the Punjab Legislature in 2004, defying the party high command.

38 The failure of AAP to put up any chief ministerial candidate may be viewed in this context, as the party did not have any leader of similar stature to take on Captain or Badal senior. Though, the other argument could be that the party leadership at the centre wanted to keep control in its own hand.

6 Lok Sabha elections in Punjab
1999–2019

After having a detailed discussion of Assembly elections in Punjab that have taken place since the cessation of militancy in the preceding section, this section discusses Lok Sabha elections that have taken place since 1999. As the ensuing discussion shows, a certain degree of commonality in the electoral trends in the state is visible whether it is the Assembly elections or the Lok Sabha elections held in the state. For one, electoral volatility has long been the trademark of the state politics whether it relates to the elections for assemblies or for Lok Sabha.

Lok Sabha elections, 1999 and 2004

The Lok Sabha elections held in 2004 were no exception as the SAD-BJP combine won 11 out of 13 Lok Sabha seats. SAD won 8 out of 10 seats it contested, with 34.3 percent of vote share. BJP won all the three seats it contested, polling at 10.5 percent. Combined the SAD-BJP vote share came to 44.8 percent of the total votes. Congress this time could only win 2 out of 11 seats it contested, polling 34.2 percent of the total votes polled. Its allies CPI and CPM drew a blank, contesting one seat each, with a meagre share of 2.6 and 1.8 percent of the votes, respectively. Mann-led SAD (Amritsar) won the remaining one seat polling 3.8 percent. It was obvious that notwithstanding the presence of minor parties (numbering 24) as well as independents, the contest mainly remained between the Congress and the SAD. Among the smaller parties, the Lok Bhalai party did well in the Ludhiana constituency as its president Balwant Singh Ramoowalia received 187,000 votes cutting into Congress votes. As a result SAD candidate Sharanjit Singh Dhillon managed to defeat Congress candidate Manish Tiwari. Dal Khalsa, another minor party in the fray supported Sarbjit Singh Khalsa, son of Beant Singh, one of the assassins of Indira Gandhi. Khalsa was a SAD (Amritsar) candidate for Bathinda. Akal Council, a party headed by Bhai Ranjit Singh, a former Akal Takht Jathedar decided not to contest the elections.[1]

Compared to the 1999 Lok Sabha elections and the more recent 2002 Assembly elections, the electoral outcome this time was a complete reversal of the electoral fortunes of the two major parties. In 1999 Lok Sabha elections, a resurgent Congress won eight seats polling at 38.4 percent point votes as against the SAD winning two seats and BJP winning one seat (the alliance won 28.6 and 9.2 percent of the total votes polled).

As discussed in the preceding section, in the 2002 Assembly elections that preceded 2004 elections, the Congress, SAD, and BJP had polled 35.8, 31.1, and 5.7 percent of the votes giving the Congress-CPI alliance 64 assembly seats compared to 44 seats won by the SAD-BJP combine. In the 2004 elections, however, the Congress won only Lok Sabha seats of Patiala and Jalandhar.

How does one explain the fact that the Congress and its allies lost the 2004 Lok Sabha elections so badly within two years of their success in the Assembly elections? Was a period of two years sufficient for anti-incumbency to set in even if one keeps in mind the volatile nature of the state's politics? What were the other factors and issues that contributed to it? Unlike the last two elections, this election witnessed a newfound unity among the Akalis. Sarb Hind Shiromani Akali Dal (SHSAD), founded by late Gurcharan Singh Tohra, had merged with the official SAD before the elections. SAD (Democratic) led by Kuldip Singh Wadala also merged with the SAD. Notably, the split in Akali votes had resulted in the loss of three seats, namely, Ropar, Patiala, and Ludhiana for the SAD-BJP alliance in the 1999 elections. At that time, SHSAD had secured more than 5 percent of the votes in the constituencies of Gurdaspur, Bathinda, and Tarn Taran, directly spoiling the chances of SAD. The exception to this was that the SAD (Amritsar) led by Mann stayed out of an all Akali party alliance. Sikh masses virtually rejected this time the party, probably because it spoke more against the Akali leadership than the Congress, thus dividing the panthic vote. Moreover, its radical agenda was no longer catching the attention of the people in a changed political climate. Congress suffered from internal dissension as Amarinder Singh and his deputy Rajinder Kaur Bhattal fought their personal battle in open. The then president of the state unit H. S. Hanspal was unable to carry with him the factions of Congress led by these two leaders due to his perceived proximity to the chief minister. Moreover, his coming from a non-Jat Sikh community (Khatri) also weakened his authority in the party matters.

SAD during its electoral campaign nailed the Congress government in the state over its failure to check the continuing deceleration of Punjab's economy. Withdrawal of free water and electricity to the farmers also came in for an attack. Captain himself on the day of the results conceded it as a contributing factor to the Congress' dismal performance. Akalis also highlighted the withdrawal of the 'Shagun' scheme for the marriage of every Scheduled castes and lower caste Christian girl. Populist schemes started by the Congress government for the progress of disadvantaged groups, such as the Rajiv Gandhi Pendu Jan Sehat Kalyan Yojna for the Scheduled castes, the Kanya Jagrity Jyoti scheme for two daughters of every Scheduled castes family, and the Jan Shri insurance scheme for Scheduled castes families living below the poverty line failed to retain the traditional support of the Scheduled castes for the Congress. Government employees were also dissatisfied with the state government's refusal to concede to their long-pending demands. Corruption was another issue flagged by opposition.

Congress during its campaign decried SAD leadership for promoting nepotism. A highly personalised campaign also witnessed the Congress taking up the issue of assets allegedly acquired by Badal family through illegal means when in power. SAD in its turn accused the Amarinder Singh government of corruption in the liquor-vending auction and in the appointment of DSPs against sports quota. Hawala charges against son of Amarinder Singh and the ongoing corruption case against Bhattal for alleged embezzlement of public funds during her chiefministership received publicity. On the other hand, the single-track, anti-corruption drive launched by the Congress government in the last two years against Akali leaders especially the Badal family did not pay electoral dividends. What also caused the Sikh voters' anguish was the Congress giving tickets in Delhi to the party candidates implicated in the anti-Sikh riots in 1984. Popular discontent with the performance of Amarinder Singh government was most glaring among the farming community. Without creating a level playing field, the opening up of the farming sector under the WTO regime has meant tremendous hardship for the erstwhile 'rich farmers' of Punjab as the input costs escalated. Promises made by the Congress to take up appropriate measures like the diversification of crops, the provision of cold storage facilities, and the setting up of agro-processing units remained mostly on paper. Under the WTO regime, increased prices of the genetically developed crop seeds added to farmers' woes. Many publicised governmental measures like farmer's income insurance scheme on pilot basis, contract farming, privatisation of farm marketing, and call centres hardly took off the ground. The Planning Commission's offer to provide Rs. 5,500 per acre as compensation for crop diversification to break the paddy-wheat nexus came too late for the Congress to cash on it. SAD also raised the issue of delayed payment for sugar cane arrears as well as irregularity in the payment of the pensions for the old under Ashirvad scheme.

Performance at the constituency level mattered. It was evident in the case of the electoral outcome in an important constituency namely Patiala. The sitting MP Preneet Kaur of the Congress and wife of Amarinder Singh overcame anti-incumbency factor and dissidence primarily because she was able to highlight her developmental efforts in the constituency, i.e. sewerage projects for the city, a 300-acre new township and flood protection project along the Ghggar River. Sukhbir Singh Badal victory over Karan Brar of Congress with the highest victory margin of over 1.36 lakh votes in Faridkot was arguably due to his relentless work in the constituency, which he lost in 1999 by a slender margin of 0.6 percent to Jagmeet Singh Brar. Badal junior, a former union minister, took credit for setting up Baba Farid University of health sciences in Faridkot, a regional centre of Punjab Technical University in Muktsar, as well as other management and IT institutes besides the establishment of power grids to improve the power supply to farmers in his constituency. Similarly, Vinod Khanna's consecutive third term win in Gurdaspur could be attributed to his role in the construction of multi-crore bridge over Beas River and the revival of Dhariwal woollen mill through a Rs 200 crore special project sanctioned by the centre. Khanna had managed to scrape past Sukhbans Kaur Bhinder of the Congress by a margin of 0.2 percent in 1999 Lok Sabha elections. Failure of Congress government to complete Laxman Canal project as promised in the earlier elections contributed to the defeat of Congress in Ferozpur where the party was hopeful this time. The only other woman candidate to win the Lok Sabha election along with Praneet Kaur was Paramjit Kaur Gulshan of SAD who won from the Bathinda constituency, defeating Kushal Bhaura, a woman candidate of Congress party. The loss of Congress candidate from Sangrur could be attributed to the BSP decision to withdraw from the fray a couple of days before the polling. Similarly, the victory of Zora Singh Mann, the SAD nominee from Ferozepur over Congress candidate Jagmeet Singh Brar, sitting MP from Faridkot, was possible because the BSP candidate Mohan Singh Phalianwala cut in to votes of Brar by bagging 101,921 votes. Brar lost by 11,539 votes despite leading in five of the nine assembly constituencies.

The verdict reflected that the electorates were not so keen on the lopsided politics of 'Badal', 'Badla' (vendetta), and 'Badli' (transfer) that boomeranged on the Amarinder Singh–led Congress government. The government's failure to address the economic woes was one of the most important factors for the failure of the Congress to take advantage of being in power in the state. SAD also publicised the increasing state's debt burden though when in power during 1997–2002, they were equally responsible for it as Badal, after becoming Chief Minister in 1997, had introduced free electricity to the farmers, including even rich farmers.

The elections continued to see the slide in the electoral fortune of the BSP as the party failed to win even a single seat. However, the party did put up a credible performance by getting impressive votes in this election, adding to the discomfort of the Congress. The incident in Talhan in Jalandhar district where there was a tussle between the Jat landed peasantry and Scheduled castes over the issue of control over the management of a gurdwara played a role in galvanising support for the BSP among the Scheduled castes. A clear-cut three-way split of votes resulted in BSP emerging as a distant third alternative. Like Akalis, the BSP also had fared poorly in 1999 as the party at the time was divided into three 'Bahujan' parties, namely, the BSP, the BSP (Ambedkar), and the Democratic Bahujan Samaj Morcha (DBSM). In 1999, the BSP had contested in three constituencies and polled at 3.8 percent of the votes. In 2004, it contested in all the 13 seats and polled at 7.7 percent of the votes.

Like in the case of earlier elections, both assembly as well as parliamentary ones, the final tally of votes revealed that a tie up with BSP would have paid rich dividends to the Congress (or for that matter SAD), which had made an attempt to have a pre-poll alliance that did not materialise in the absence of any national alliance between the two parties. A Congress-BSP combine would definitely have won the seats in Ropar, Phillaur,

Ferozepur, and Sangrur. BSP came third in all the constituencies except Tarn Taran, Ludhiana, Sangrur, and Bathinda. As the results showed, BSP at that time still had a strong base among Scheduled castes, especially in the Doaba region, besides certain parts of Malwa such as Ferozepur. If the BSP could get rid of factionalism at that time, it was probably capable of repeating its 1998 elections results when it had emerged as a strong third force. It had then secured more than 40 percent of votes polled in Hoshiarpur, Firozepur and Phillaur. Incidents of atrocities committed on the Scheduled castes in the absence of any strict implementation of the SC and ST Act, the failure to fulfil the demand of redistribution of the village common land property ('shamlat') among the Scheduled castes, and the continuing decline in real wages—not necessarily in the daily rates of agricultural labourers in the face of oversupply of rural labour in the form of migrant Bihari labourers and no great increase of industrial employment in urban areas—all ensured that even the traditional Scheduled castes voters did not vote for the Congress in this election (Mendelssohn and Vicziany, 2000, p. 170, 175).

The NES'2004 post-poll survey revealed that two major factors seemed to go in favour of the SAD-BJP alliance. First, the alliance benefited from a positive evaluation of BJP-led NDA government at the centre. Second, dissatisfaction with the performance of Congress government in the state also helped. When asked to compare the performance of the present Congress government with the previous SAD-BJP government, 43 percent of respondents interviewed in CSDS post-poll survey rated Badal-led SAD-BJP coalition government better than the Amarinder Singh–led Congress government. That performance mattered was clear by the fact that majority of those who rated highly the performance of the previous SAD-BJP government in the state also voted for the alliance. What further helped the alliance was the positive appraisal of the BJP-led NDA government at the centre as 59 percent of respondents interviewed were either somewhat or fully satisfied. Forty-eight percent of respondents wanted to give another chance to Vajpayee's leadership as compared to 30 percent who had a definitive contrary view. On the leadership issue, in a national election, the SAD-BJP combine did better, as 45 percent preferred Atal Bihari Vajpayee as the next Prime Minister as compared to Sonia Gandhi, who received the support of 31 percent. It helped the Akalis that Badal was preferred as the next chief minister by 30 percent as against Amarinder Singh who was the choice of 27 percent. Only 5 percent of the respondents approved of Rajinder Kaur Bhattal, a prominent dissident and self-proclaimed candidate for chief ministership in the Congress. Responses to questions on the performance of the Congress government in the state reflected adverse perceptions. On the issues of law and order, condition of roads, irrigation facilities, supply of electricity, and combating corruption, only about one-third of the respondents thought that the situation had improved during the Congress regime. A large majority thought that it had either deteriorated or remained as before. Similarly, in this largely agrarian state, 31 percent thought that the situation of farmers had deteriorated. Despite the smear campaign marked by personalised political acrimony, corruption charges against Badal did not seem to stick, as only 34 percent either completely or somewhat believed in the validity of the cases filed against him. In the overall context of the measures taken by Amarinder Singh government to curb corruption, half the respondents thought that the situation had either remained same as before or had deteriorated (Kumar, 2004a).

The survey revealed the primacy of local over national issue as a significant 57 percent of Punjabi voters either fully or somewhat agreed with the idea that loyalty to the immediate region mattered first and then the country came. Forty percent either fully or somewhat agreed that, compared to national parties, regional/local parties could provide better governance in states. This perception might be one factor for SAD to thrive in Punjab. As for the support bases of the parties, the survey data showed Congress ahead of the SAD-BJP alliance in urban localities. Caste wise voting pattern shows that the Congress trailed the SAD-BJP alliance among all the social groups except the Scheduled castes. In terms of class categories, Congress had a lead over SAD-BJP only among very poor voters (Kumar, 2004a).

The NES data as compared to the Punjab assembly election study—2002 data (Kumar and Kumar, 2002) referred to in the preceding section revealed that reversal in the electoral fortunes of SAD-BJP combine and the Congress in 2004 was not merely a quantitative one but was related to the performance of the incumbent governments both at the centre and in the state level and the consequent adverse perceptions of the people.

2009 Lok Sabha elections

Typical of the 'Punjab tradition' of cyclical electoral verdicts, Punjab witnessed the resurgence of the Congress at the cost of the SAD-BJP alliance in 2009 Lok Sabha elections. The electoral figures, however, also showed the close nature of bi-polar contest (again a constant feature in Punjab politics) as only a slender lead in terms of votes[2] polled enabled Congress to march ahead over the SAD-BJP combine in terms of number of seats won ('How India Voted', *The Hindu*, 2009, May 26). The number was much greater, if referred to the number of assembly constituencies segments where Congress took lead in as many as 65 assembly constituencies segments as against 44 constituencies having Congress legislators. BJP has always suffered more compared to SAD whenever the alliance loses any election.[3] While the core social constituency, the land-owning rural Jat Sikhs voted for SAD in sizable numbers, BJP could not receive support from its traditional base among the urban voters, who turned to the Congress this time.

As for other parties in the fray, BSP continued to register poor performance despite the significant presence of the Scheduled castes (SC) voters, which is 29 percent of state's population as against the national average of 16 percent as per the 2001 census. The party could mark its electoral presence only in Ferozepur and Hoshiarpur (reserved) constituencies. This was so because the Congress retained its support base among the Scheduled castes having different religious allegiance, i.e. Hindu, Christian, and Sikh, particularly in the Doaba region where there is a large concentration of these castes. In addition, the gradual slide of the CPI and the CPM, the erstwhile electoral allies of Congress until 2007 Assembly elections, helped the party in winning the 'secular' left-leaning vote.

Decline of BSP in electoral terms since its impressive performance in 1997 Assembly elections when it won three seats in alliance with SAD, decisively helped the Congress, which has always had a decent support base among the Scheduled castes, despite the SC having different religious allegiance, i.e. Hindu, Christian, and Sikh, particularly in the Doaba region where there is a large concentration of these castes. In addition, the gradual slide of the CPI and the CPM, the erstwhile electoral allies of Congress until 2007 Assembly elections, helped the party in winning the 'secular' vote.

As for the record, the total number of candidates who contested elections was an all-time high 218 out of whom 113 were independents, whereas the rest were represented by 30 parties including SAD (Amritsar) led by Simranjit Singh Mann and Lok Bhalai Party led by Balwant Singh Ramoowalia.[4] Punjab also maintained the tradition of high electoral participation in the state, which at 70.4 percent was once again more than the national average. Such a high percentage was commendable and so was the fact that these elections, conducted in two phases for the first time in the history of the post-1966 Punjab, turned out to be one of the most peaceful elections ever witnessed in the state.[5]

As for the record, total number of candidates who contested elections was an all-time high 218, including 113 independents, whereas the rest were represented by 30 parties including SAD (Amritsar) led by Simranjit Singh Mann and the Lok Bhalai Party led by Balwant Singh Ramoowalia.[6] Punjab also maintained the tradition of high electoral participation in the state, which at 70.4 percent was once again more than the national average. Such a high percentage could also be attributed to the fact that these elections, conducted in two phases for the first time in the history of the post-1966 Punjab, turned out to be one of the most peaceful elections ever witnessed in the state.[7] Looking back at 2009 elections, the following features could be discerned.

First, Punjab like many other constituent states like Andhra Pradesh, Karnataka, and Maharashtra witnessed major territorial changes in the constituencies' profiles due to the fourth delimitation exercise. The changed electoral map in the state saw the number of the reserved constituencies (for Scheduled castes) going up from three to four.[8] Erstwhile constituencies of Phillaur and Ropar, reserved for Scheduled castes, ceased to exist. Constituencies of Jalandhar, Hoshiarpur, and Faridkot were now reserved for Scheduled castes. Bathinda constituency became unreserved post-delimitation with minor territorial change, paving the way for two politically powerful families of Congress and SAD to stake their claim. Fatehgarh Sahib became a new reserved constituency by carving out territory of Ropar. Another constituency carved out of the erstwhile Ropar constituency was Anandpur Sahib. Part of the Phillaur constituency merged into the Jalandhar reserved constituency. Another new general constituency created was Khadoor Sahib, named Tarn Taran before delimitation. After the delimitation, large tracts from Ferozepur and Jalandhar became part of Khadoor Sahib, bringing in more urban population. Another constituency that underwent major territorial change was Ludhiana, which now became 90 percent urban. Faridkot was another such constituency which saw major territorial change. These changes did have their impact over the electoral outcome as would be discussed later while taking up constituency wise analysis.

Second, there were as many as four women successful candidates in the 2009 elections, which is unprecedented for a state that has had a negligible presence of women representatives in the public bodies and has the dubious distinction of having one of the most adverse sex ratios in the country. Two of these four elected women representatives, however, belonged to political families of the state and as such their candidacy had nothing to do with their gender.

Third, these elections also marked the 'controlled experiment' carried out by Rahul Gandhi in terms of assigning party tickets to as many as three relatively young and inexperienced candidates who had excelled in the organisational elections carried out within the state unit of Youth Congress a year before. Two among them actually managed to win, a significant development, notwithstanding the fact that they too came from political families.

A notable feature of the 2009 elections was the regional variations in the electoral performance in these elections as compared to the earlier one. The BJP-SAD combine was wiped out in the Doaba region (Jalandhar and Hoshiarpur), which has a sizable presence of Scheduled castes voters. Significantly, in the 2007 Assembly elections it was SAD-BJP alliance, which had swept the region by winning eight out of nine assembly segments while the Congress could retain only Nakodar constituency. SAD, however, recovered its position in the Malwa region comprising of Ludhiana, Anandpur Sahib, Fatehgarh Sahib, Sangrur, Patiala, Faridkot, Firozepur, and Bathinda constituencies by winning two seats. In 2007 Assembly elections, SAD had suffered heavily in this region, which was attributed primarily to the decision of the Dera Sacha Sauda, which has had a large following among the Scheduled castes and backward castes in the region, to support the Congress.[9] What helped the Akalis this time was the neutral stand taken by the Dera[10] and the success of recently introduced BT cotton seeds, which considerably checked the farmers' indebtedness. Privileging the Malwa region in terms of developmental schemes and projects, allegedly at the cost of the other two regions, was the most important factor. During the campaign, Congress raised the issue of regional discrimination. The other two seats for the SAD came from Majha region (Khadoor Sahib and Gurdaspur), called the 'cradle of Sikhism' due to the presence of the Sikh shrines, whereas its ally BJP could win only one seat of Amritsar (Kumar and Sekhon, 2009).

Congress victories in the constituencies spread across all the three regions of the state was notable considering the fact that Congress did not win any seat from Majha region and managed only one seat each in Doaba and Malwa in the 2004 Lok Sabha elections. In a similar vein, SAD fared much better in the Malwa region from where Congress had won as many as 41 assembly seats out of total 63 constituencies in the 2007 Assembly elections.

The most keenly fought electoral battle in the 2009 elections took place in the constituencies of Bathinda and Patiala, both belonging to the Malwa region, where the two most powerful families of former and present chief ministers threw their weight in a battle for prestige and one-upmanship, typical of the state where kinship remains major determinant of electoral politics. Harsimrat Kaur, the daughter-in-law of the incumbent Chief Minister Parkash Singh Badal and wife of the SAD President Sukhbir Badal managed to defeat Raninder Singh, son of the former Chief Minister Amarinder Singh with what turned out to be the highest margin of victory in the state. The majority of Akali votes came from rural assembly segments confirming the rural support base of the party as revealed in CSDS-NES survey data. What gave a head start to Kaur in her in-laws' home constituency was her clean image built upon her activism in the years preceding the elections when she took up environmental issues, in a state where ecological degradation is a reality, and also a long-term initiative called 'Nanhi Chhan' (the little shade) to save the girl child from widely prevalent feticide. In the neighbouring Patiala constituency Preneet Kaur, wife of Amarinder Singh, won against Prem Singh Chandumajra despite an all-out campaign launched by Sukhbir Badal against her. Besides being a royal belonging to the former princely state, Kaur also benefited from the internal dissension led by Surjit Singh Barnala and Late Gurcharan Singh Tohra factions that erupted within the SAD in the aftermath of the sudden death of Captain Kanwaljit Singh, a senior leader who had represented for a long time the Banur assembly segment. The now reserved constituency of Hoshiarpur in Doaba region, which has the highest percentage of Schedule castes population in Punjab, also witnessed a close contest where the BJP candidate Som Paul lost to his Congress rival Santosh Chaudhary, chairperson of the National Commission for Safai Karamcharis, by a slender margin of 366 votes. One of the reasons for the Congress candidate's success was her being a veteran leader and former Member of Parliament from a now defunct Phillaur (reserved) constituency, whereas the BJP candidate was considered relatively unknown in the area and politically inexperienced, having just resigned from civil service. In Jalandhar (reserved) constituency, dubbed as the 'political capital' of the Doaba region, Mohinder Singh Kaypee, then state Congress President, defeated Akali candidate Hans Raj Hans, a Sufi singer. Kaypee victory could be attributed to his strong political background and rich administrative experience. The defeat of Hans Raj Hans was also partly because the Balmiki community he belongs to has been a traditional supporter of the Congress. Another constituency, which witnessed a close fight, was Amritsar where the incumbent BJP candidate Navjot

Singh Sidhu, a Jat Sikh, managed to scrape through against Congress candidate Om Prakash Soni mainly due to the support he received from the five rural assembly constituencies falling within the Lok Sabha constituency, the traditional strongholds of the Akalis. The result showed a definitive shift in the rural-urban voting pattern as the Congress candidate led in all the four urban assembly constituencies, which went in favour of the BJP in the 2007 Assembly elections. These constituencies have a large number of upper caste Hindus, considered traditional supporters of BJP. Congress projecting Manmohan Singh, whose family had roots in the city, as its candidate for Prime Minister worked well with the urban voters. It was, however, also true that they felt let down by the BJP for not being able to ensure equal treatment to the urban electorates who suffered from electricity cuts and the absence of any relief to the local industries despite being in the coalition government. Besides, the SAD was able to mobilise rural support under the leadership of Bikramjit Singh Majithia, brother-in-law of Sukhbir Badal. In addition, Sidhu's clean image helped whereas Soni faced allegations of being soft on the drug peddlers and liquor lobby in the borderland area. Similar allegations also contributed to the defeat of Congress candidate Rana Gurjit Singh, a sugar and liquor baron in the area, at the hand of Akali candidate Rattan Singh Ajnala in newly created Khadoor Sahib, earlier known as Tarn Taran before the fourth delimitation exercise. The Seminaries of Radha Soami Dera and Damdami Taksal, who preach absenteeism from alcohol, were not positively inclined to Rana. Except in 1992 elections boycotted by the Akalis, Congress has never won from this Sikh dominated borderland constituency, once infested by militancy. Gurdaspur was another touch and go constituency where sitting BJP candidate Vinod Khanna was unable to defeat the Congress candidate Pratap Singh Bajwa, a former Congress minister. Unlike the other two border belt Sikh-majority constituencies of Majha region, i.e. Amritsar and Khadur Sahib, Gurdaspur is a Hindu majority constituency. Congress gained from the development work that took place in the area with the efforts of Aswani Kumar, Union minister of State for Industries, like setting up a 63 Crore Machine tool cluster project, a collection centre for the proposed Mega Food Park and Polytechnics. Khanna, a three-time MP was presented as an 'outsider'. The process of delimitation made a clear and determined impact on the outcome of this constituency. The two assembly segments namely Qadian and Batala, the area Bajwa belongs to, were added to Gurdaspur, whereas the Mukerian assembly segment, the BJP stronghold and from where Khanna had a massive lead last time against Congress candidate Sukhbans Kaur Bhinder due to his being credited with building the much-needed bridge over Beas, was excluded from it and added to Hoshiarpur Lok Sabha constituency. Mukerian was the only assembly segment where the BJP candidate took lead where it had sitting MLAs. Ferozepur contest saw the defeat of Congress candidate Jagmeet Singh Brar, who had also lost narrowly in the past two elections, respectively, from Faridkot and Firozepur. Mandate for Sher Singh Ghubaiya of SAD was primarily due to wholehearted support from his own numerically strong Rai Sikh farming community settled after post-partition migration in the border areas. Post-partition, Rai Sikhs have faced tremendous hardship due to the barbed wiring and high voltage 'cobra wire' by armed forces and occasional breakouts of hostility between India and Pakistan. Ravneet Singh Bittu, grandson of former Chief Minister Beant Singh and first democratically elected President of the Punjab Youth Congress (PYC) in Anandpur Sahib Constituency defeated Daljeet Singh Cheema, political advisor to Badal senior as well as secretary-cum-spokesperson of SAD. While other Rahul Gandhi nominee Sukhwinder Singh Danny, son of former minister Sardul Singh and the first democratically elected (and not nominated) vice-president of the Punjab Youth Congress (PYC), lost from Faridkot; Vijay Inder Singla, former PYC President won from Sangrur. Junior Gandhi not only actively campaigned but also made conscious efforts to galvanise party machinery in support of these first-time candidates who were preferred over veterans like Ambika Soni. Singla defeated Akali veteran Sukhdev Singh Dhindsa as well as Simranjeet Singh Mann, the President of SAD (Amritsar) and Balwant Singh Ramoowalia, Lok Bhalai Party leader. Manish Tewari was another relatively younger candidate who this time could win from Ludhiana against Gurcharan Singh Galib of SAD. Predominantly urban character of the constituency after delimitation as well as the presence of a large number of migrant populations from Uttar Pradesh and Bihar in the industrial town of Ludhiana went in Congress' favour. Sukhdev Singh Libra, who had defied the SAD and voted for Manmohan Singh government on a no confidence motion, managed to win Fatehgarh Sahib reserved constituency on Congress ticket against Akali candidate Charanjit Singh Atwal, deputy speaker of the 14th Lok Sabha. Libra ran a campaign in the name of Manmohan Singh, asking the voters to vote for Congress (Kumar and Sekhon, 2009).

The dismal performance of SAD-BJP combine was primarily due to the non-performance of the BJP. Ironically, BJP had secured an unprecedented 19 seats in 2007 Assembly elections boosting the coalition performance. SAD unlike BJP in 2009 elections somehow managed to keep its vote share, if not the seats, intact in rural Punjab and helped BJP in retaining Amritsar Constituency ensuring rural votes.

Let us look for possible explanations for the SAD-BJP debacle. CSDS-NES Punjab post-poll survey findings showed that SAD, traditionally viewed as a Panthic party, managed to retain its traditional support base among rural Sikhs. The pro-farmer image of SAD was evident in popular psyche. When asked about the party being most capable in solving the agrarian crisis in Punjab that afflicts post–Green Revolution Punjab economy, 38 percent of the respondents named SAD as compared to 32 percent who named Congress. BJP stood at poor third with 3 percent, affirming the pro-urban image of the party. A decisive factor that went in favour of the Congress was a significant 6 percent of vote shift in the urban localities in party's favour whereas BJP-SAD suffered a decline of 3 percent. The survey made it clear that the long-term alliance between SAD and BJP was beneficial to both of them as left to contest alone; it would be the Congress, which would be having an upper hand with its wider support base bridging the rural-urban or Hindu-Sikh divide (Kumar and Sekhon, 2009).[11]

What explained the shift in the urban voters' voting pattern against the ruling coalition in this particular election? First, dissatisfaction of the urban voters with the SAD-BJP ruling coalition was evident in this particular election particularly about giving freebies to the rural population, particularly cost-free electricity and water to the farm sector whereas the urban cities and the industrial sectors continue to face acute power crisis, despite publicised electoral assurances. Congress government also continued subsidised power to the farmers, but it was the SAD which was considered responsible for starting the trend of heavy subsidies. Second, respondents viewed the BJP as playing a second fiddle to the SAD, having no significant influence over the policy-making process and being unable to safeguard the interests of the traders and the industrial houses—its traditional voters. Party's core voters who had high expectations after its impressive success in the 2007 elections felt betrayed. Third, tension between the alliance partners was evident as the two parties contested separately in 2008 local elections. Fourth, despite having shared power in the post-1997 state for eight years, BJP was yet to have strong state-level leadership and develop an agenda that could capture the imagination of the urban electorates on a consistent basis. The success of SAD in retaining its rural support base largely in post-militancy Punjab may be linked to the party's efforts to assert its pro-farmer credentials. In its 2009 election manifesto, SAD tried to shed its pro-urban bias visible in the party manifesto released on the eve of 2007 assembly election manifesto, i.e. emphasis on urban development, world class airports, roads, SEZ. This time, SAD promised soft farm loans after waiving off all pending liabilities in the agriculture sector. The party also promised to provide highly subsidised diesel and create a Special Corpus Fund to provide adequate relief during natural calamities. It also proposed introduction of income insurance for the farm sector, 50 percent subsidy on new warehouses to speed up storage and movement of food grains, easy loans to encourage food processing and other farm-related industry in Punjab, and a single-zone system for farm products, especially food grains (Kumar and Sekhon, 2009).

The 2009 elections saw for the first time the emergence of Sukhbir Badal as leading the electoral campaign of the SAD, even as his father remained the face of the campaign. Naturally, the question was about the electoral impact of the elevation of Sukhbir Singh Badal as the Deputy Chief Minister (despite the demand of the same post by the state BJP unit). In the CSDS-NES survey data relating to the question regarding the respondents' choice about chief minister for Punjab; merely 2 percent preferred Badal junior[12] to his father who was preferred by 27 percent. The candidacy of Captain, the chief election campaigner for Congress, got support of 33 percent, confirming his stature as the tallest Congress leader in the state.[13]

While referring to the national level effect, what now seems improbable, indeed the 'Manmohan factor' held greater appeal to the Punjabi voters and helped the Congress. The survey findings showed that 41 as against 24 percent of voters thought that Manmohan Singh was declared as the Congress Prime Ministerial candidate was aimed at wooing the Sikh voters. Significantly, there was a 5 percent shift in the Sikh voters' preference for Congress as compared to the 2004 elections as per NES data. When asked about their preference about the next Prime Minister of India, 43 percent of the respondents from Punjab preferred Manmohan Singh to L. K. Advani, who was preferred only by 13 percent. The personal preference did affect the electoral outcome as 75 percent of those who preferred Manmohan Singh did vote for Congress while 19 percent of them voted for BJP-SAD, whereas in the case of Advani, 94 percent of those who preferred him voted for the BJP-SAD alliance.

Given the fact that it was an Amarinder Singh–led Congress government which had got a resolution passed unanimously terminating the river water treaty by the state assembly, it went to the credit of the party. Decline of the BSP over the years became once again evident in the survey. The survey findings revealed that less than 8 percent of the voters belonging to different social and economic categories thought that the BSP in comparison to BJP, SAD, and Congress could do the best for the betterment of the Scheduled castes in the state. It was an advantage to Congress as supported by survey data as 35 percent of the respondents considered the party better than the rest. Congress also got 62 percent support of the Scheduled castes voters interviewed in 2009 as compared to merely 48 percent in the 2004 elections. Thus the Congress, after losing ground to BSP in the 1997 and 2002 elections, seemed to recover its traditional voters.

As mentioned previously, a recurrent theme interweaving most of the studies of electoral politics in recent Punjab has been the phenomenon designated as a 'shift in the political agenda'. This election also witnessed the prioritisation of the politico-economic issues over the ethno-religious issues. The contention that, by reinventing their agendas, the parties were able to recast their image and recapture the legitimacy and relevance lost during the days of militant violence found resonance in the NES' 2009 survey findings. In response to the question as to which party would be best for maintaining good relations between Hindus and Sikhs in this two-community state, Congress received support of 34 percent of the respondents as compared to the 27 percent support received by SAD and 6 percent for BJP. It indicated that Congress, once decried as a 'Hindu party' in the post-Bluestar days, was able to make a comeback as a party with secular credentials. SAD also moved away from being viewed primarily as a 'panthic party'. In its historic Moga declaration, adopted on 14 April 1995, the party committed itself to a more secular politics based on 'Punjab, Punjabi and Punjabiat' besides panth (Kumar, 2004, p. 1519). To quote from the historic document: 'the spirit of Punjabiat would be strengthened so that these matters get projected as common problems of the entire Punjabis rather than a section thereof' (cited in Singh, 1995, p. 4). Trying to get rid of being dubbed as a 'Jat Sikh party', SAD started putting up the Hindus and Scheduled castes as the party candidates since the 2007 Assembly elections and also assigned them roles in the party's organisation.

SAD continued to refrain from mentioning the Anandpur Sahib resolutions in its manifesto or during the campaign, ostensibly under pressure from BJP, but also for the party's sincere desire to broaden its support base on a long-term basis across the communities.[14] Similarly, rather than going for confrontation with the centre, the party simply asked for greater autonomy for states while condemning the 'unitarian mindset'. In a sign of convergence of political agenda, SAD, followed by state unit of Congress, also reiterated its commitment to continue its peaceful democratic struggle for inclusion of Chandigarh[15] and other Punjabi-speaking areas back into Punjab and sought settlement of the inter-state river water issue on the basis of nationally and internationally accepted riparian principle.

The substantive issues like the agrarian crisis confronting post–Green Revolution Punjab hardly received any critical attention in the policy domain like in the earlier elections. If the SAD-BJP was able to retain power post-2012, it showed that populism[16] reigned supreme despite the government facing a huge debt burden.[17]

Summing up the saga of the 2009 election, it was like earlier elections in the sense that it hardly held any promise of a cataclysmic shift in the electoral politics of the beleaguered state. The gains or losses of the two contending parties were more in the form of an election-specific development or in a more general sense a result of routine electoral cycle. The outcome was to be viewed primarily as a negative vote by the electorates disillusioned with the non-performance of the SAD-BJP government and in no way signified long-term gains of the Congress in the state. The electoral verdict in 2012 when SAD-BJP combine bucked the trend by retaining power showed that efforts to bring about development, howsoever inadequate they may be, could win handsome electoral reward as voters' expectation levels remain fairly low.[18]

2014 Lok Sabha elections[19]

The 2014 Lok Sabha elections in Punjab[20] received much attention both in the media as well as in academic world due to the unexpected electoral success of the debutant AAP. The party, which had been contested from virtually all over India after its impressive debut in 2012 Assembly elections in Delhi, could win only four seats and all these seats happened to be from Punjab.[21] Punjab was in fact among the few relatively bigger states in India, as it deviated from the national trend in favour of the BJP riding on 'Modi wave'.[22] Electorates in the state denied any significant electoral gain to BJP. The long-standing ruling SAD-BJP combine in the state managed to add only one seat to its 2009 elections tally. The alliance won six parliamentary seats with SAD winning four and the BJP winning two seats, respectively, with three seats going to the Congress. Significantly, while Congress only lost seats as compared to 2009 elections, all these three parties suffered in terms of loss of votes.

Electoral success of AAP in Punjab was exceptional. The fledgling party barely had come into existence in October 2012 in faraway Delhi, riding on the popularity wave of an Anna Hazare–led 'India' against Corruption movement. The movement was confined to mostly metropolitan cities and had witnessed essentially the involvement of urban middle classes. As per pollsters' opinion, the party was supposed to have some influence only in Haryana besides Delhi,[23] where it had formed a short-lived minority government after 2013 Assembly elections with outside support of the Congress (Kumar, 2014b).[24]

AAP success in 2014 elections seemed to have long-term electoral implications for the borderland state, marking any significant shift in the state's politics in an institutional/systemic sense, if not in terms of electoral agenda. After a long gap of 17 years that witnessed three Lok Sabha elections, 2014 elections marked a break from what has long become an established bi-polar polity in the state, as in all these parliamentary elections the seats were shared among the three parties namely Congress, BJP, and SAD. It was in the 2014 elections that AAP contesting for the first time in the state with first-time contestants (with the exception of Bhagwant Mann who had fought and lost the 2012 Assembly elections on a PPP ticket), some of whom came with an impeccable record of public service like a practicing doctor in Patiala, Dharamvir Gandhi. AAP not only managed to secure nearly one-fourth of the total votes polled in the state, but also won one third of the Lok Sabha seats. On the strength of its performance, the party emerged as a viable third alternative for the state's electorates (Kumar, 2014b).

AAP success in the state was also remarkable, as it was not confined to a particular electoral region. In Punjab, the presence of the parties except the Congress and the SAD has been confined to particular region, CPI and CPM to Malwa region and the BSP to Doaba region. AAP to its credit received significant support in all the three electoral regions of Punjab. However, the party's success in terms of winning the seats came only from the electorally most important region of Malwa. Malwa region comprises of as many as 69 out of 117 assembly constituencies in the state and is considered a stronghold of the SAD due to the tradition support of the big landed peasantry in the state to the party (Verma, 1999, p. 51). It was in the Malwa region that the AAP registered all its victories in the constituencies of Sangrur, Faridkot, Fatehgarh Sahib, and Patiala with an overall vote share of 29 percent. Significantly, the party did not fare badly in the other nine constituencies as well (Kumar and Sekhon, 2014). The party finished third in eight constituencies and in seven of these eight constituencies, it polled more votes than the margin of victory of the winning candidate, thus leaving its distinct impact over the final electoral outcome.

Electoral success of AAP defied the conventional wisdom about the electoral politics, both state-specific and also in general. First, AAP succeeded in marking its electoral presence with untried new faces as candidates, as mentioned previously, taking on successfully the established parties with a proven steady social support base and recognised state-wide leadership, not forgetting the vast human and material resources at their command, meant to 'influence' the electoral choices of the people in 'Punjab tradition'. Second, AAP as a political party also lacked in terms of the prerequisites which are widely accepted as essential for electoral success anywhere in an electoral democracy, like a developed organisational structure, an established state-level leadership, and a coherent agenda/ideology, to be viewed as a credible alternative. Third, being a debutant party it obviously also did/could not have a traditional social support base formed, as has been the case with the long-standing parties in the state. Fourth, there was a lack of 'winnability factor' going against the AAP at the time of the poll as those who voted for the party hardly expected the party candidate to win at least in Punjab.

The exceptionality factor holds when one finds that all these factors held true as the AAP fared very badly in all other states,[25] where it contested except in Punjab, as mentioned previously. It was also in the sense that in the 2014 elections, despite the 'Modi wave', almost all the established 'regionalist' parties like All India Dravida Kadgam, Telangana Rashtriya Samiti, All India Trinamool Congress, Biju Janata Dal, YSR Congress, and Telugu Desham Party, to name a few, did well (Kailash, 2014, p. 68). Ruling SAD, the second-oldest political party in India, with a distinctive regionalist agenda, however, suffered electorally in terms of votes polled despite having a long-term alliance with a polity-wide party like the BJP, armed this time with 'Modi advantage'.[26]

Related to the 'exceptional' success of AAP was the question about the repeated failure on the part of the Congress to cash on a very visible anti-incumbency factor at the local level against the incumbent SAD-BJP government, which was in power for seven years. The question became important because, with the exception of the 2012 Assembly elections, anti-incumbency always remained a decisive factor in post-1966 Punjab. Was it simply that the AAP benefitted from double anti-incumbency that harmed both the Congress and the BJP, or were there additional factors that led to an unexpected verdict?

Looking back at electoral verdict in the state in a comparative mode, one can very well argue that unlike in most states of the north especially the Hindi-speaking ones, the 'Modi wave' failed to sweep across the state despite the mammoth efforts of the ruling combine to project Modi rather than the Chief Minister Badal senior through the election materials distributed and the advertisements put up in the print and electronic media. The seeming lack of 'Modi wave' was most visible in the case of high-profile Amritsar seat where the BJP-SAD alliance suffered a humiliating defeat as Arun Jaitely, one of the senior-most BJP national leader and close confidant of Modi, suffered a massive defeat at the hand of Captain Amarinder Singh, former Congress chief minister of the state by a massive margin despite the projection of Jaitely as the close confidant of Modi and a rally addressed by Modi in the city. Amritsar, the holiest seat of the Sikhs, is also considered the citadel of SAD in recent years as two powerful political families in the state namely Majithias and Kairons belong to the Majha region. Though the SAD-BJP combine increased its number of seats, the combined vote share came down compared to previous election.

What saved the SAD-BJP combine from a complete rout? First, it was the 'famed' ability of the SAD president and then deputy Chief Minister Sukhbir Badal to 'manage' the elections with the usual advantages that come from being in power for a long time. Second, the division of anti-SAD vote between the Congress and the AAP helped. It was reminiscent of 2012 elections when 5 per cent vote polled in favour of the PPP had caused Congress defeat. Third, the projection of Modi as the developmental leader in a state helped especially among the young voters.[27] Fourth, women turnout was higher than the men like in the Assembly elections in 2012 (79.1 percent against 78.1 percent). CSDS-NES data showed that the women voted in larger percentages for SAD in both elections as they seemed to have greater faith in the party to continue the populist schemes.

As for the Congress, candidacy of the senior state-level Congress leaders like Partap Singh Bajwa, then state party president, Sunil Jakhar, leader of the Congress Legislative party along with Captain Amarinder Singh did come together, putting a temporary break to the inner-party feuds. The party candidates, most being senior party leaders, seemed to contest elections for their own political survival confining themselves to their own constituency, hardly showing any intent or effort to synergise their collective efforts for the party's overall gain. The internal feud for supremacy within the state unit of the party was well exploited by opposition parties to spoil the image of party. The publicised scams and visible institutional inertia that plagued the UPA-II government harmed the party. Memory of poor governance under the Amarinder Singh–led Congress government in the state during 2007–2012 meant that the party could not take advantage of the lack of performance of the SAD-BJP government in an election where the local issues dominated. Congress also failed to gain from its alliance with Manpreet Badal's Punjab Peoples Party or from the continued decline of the BSP whose loss of the Scheduled castes support base actually helped AAP and to some extent SAD, as revealed in the CSDS-NES data.

Lokniti post-poll survey showed that the leadership factor helped AAP. The impressive electoral performance of AAP was partly due to the popularity of Arvind Kejriwal.[28] Credentials of party candidates also helped the party. AAP candidates had clean and secular public images, most of them were 'amateur' politicians in the sense that they dabbled into electoral politics for the first time though as professionals/artists they enjoyed peoples' goodwill on the strength of their impeccable records of community service. Here they were, pitted against what in the public eyes were the 'professional' politicians, many of them tainted and held responsible or even culpable in the people's perception of the steady decline in the economic fortunes of the state as well as widespread social evils and crimes (Kumar, 2014b).

Arguably, it was also the critical issues afflicting the state's society and economy, raised successfully with fervour during the campaign, which helped the AAP electorally. AAP having the advantage of being a first-timer in the fray and none of its candidates being in public office in the past, could credibly raised the usual issues of unemployment, price-rise, corruption, agrarian crisis, suicides of farmers, and marginalisation of small and poor peasantry. Among the issues raised, the party focused specifically on the widespread menace of drugs, blaming the political leadership of the state cutting across the party line, as well as the successive governments for criminally conniving with the drug mafia and systematically ruining the youth of the state. The drug menace has been the grim reality of the state for almost a decade now. However, none of the parties' leadership had made it an electoral issue. It gave an opportunity to the AAP leadership to put the blame squarely on both the Congress and the SAD-BJP combine for the dismal situation in the state and gain electorally even as the Congress also tried feebly to capitalise on the issue, taking its cue from the AAP leaders.[29] The AAP leaders could also voice against the alleged monopoly of the ruling party politicians and businesspersons close to the seat of power over the sand and gravel, liquor, cable, and transport with much greater credibility than the Congress.

True to their style of campaign, which included the use of social media to connect to the youth, the AAP leaders publically named the important members of the ruling SAD, including the ones in cabinet, who according to them were allegedly complicit in the liquor-drug and construction and presided over transport mafias. The wealth amassed by the ruling combine leaders including the top leadership, very much in the domain of public knowledge thanks to the affidavits filed by the candidates in the recent elections, was also a major issue raised in the elections. The luxurious life styles of the lawmakers at the expense of public exchequer even as the state government remains in dire financial straits also came up for ridicule by the AAP leaders during the campaign.

Lokniti post-poll survey data confirmed that there was no 'Modi wave' sweeping the state. Narendra Modi, however, had a clear lead over the Congress party contender Rahul Gandhi as Prime Ministerial candidate, thus damaging the Congress prospect especially in the constituencies where the SAD was on weaker ground. While 16 percent of the respondents interviewed preferred Rahul Gandhi as the Prime Minister of India after the elections, 25 percent preferred Modi. More significantly, Kejriwal had a slight edge over Gandhi in decimal terms by receiving the support of 16 percent of the respondents interviewed during the survey. The respondents thought that, compared to Modi and Rahul Gandhi, Kejriwal was more trustworthy and capable of tackling corruption. An anti-incumbency factor was very much there against the Congress also due to the party heading the coalition government at the centre. It was evident in the form of a sharp decline of support for fellow Punjabi Manmohan Singh, outgoing Prime Minister, as a significant 49.4 percent of the respondents interviewed were partially/fully dissatisfied with the performance of the UPA government. AAP gained at the cost of both the Congress as well as the SAD-BJP alliance as both contending rivals suffered from anti-incumbency factor. The data revealed that 13 percent of traditional Congress supporters and 17 percent of SAD-BJP supporters voted this time for the AAP. AAP performance was particularly noteworthy among marginal social categories. As per the data, while SAD and BSP received 19 and 4 percent of Scheduled castes votes polled, AAP received the maximum 21 percent of the votes. Also in a state where the youth constitute a significant percentage of voters, 40 percent of the young voters interviewed during the survey said that they had voted for the new party.

Survey findings supported the argument that one of the reasons for the AAP success was that the party was ahead of other parties in raising the issues and problems in these elections, which were considered the most important issues confronting the state. The survey confirmed that drug menace (58.7 percent) in the state along with price rise (27 percent) and corruption (18 percent) were the most important electoral issues identified by the electorates interviewed during the survey. Other important issues were farmer's suicides, soaring price of sand and gravel, monopoly over transport and liquor trade, recently levied property tax in the cities, controversial role of halqa-in-charge dominating police along with goondagardi/dhakkashahi of ground level cadres of ruling alliance, and increasing lawlessness and sense of insecurity among women in the state, among others. The AAP-led anti-corruption campaign did have its resonance among the masses as high as 82 percent of the respondents considered UPA government corrupt while 29.2 percent were of the view that UPA regime was responsible for the price rise. Ironically, what seemed like a classic case of pot calling the kettle black in the eyes of the electorates, the SAD-BJP was also vociferous about the issue, even as the state government was considered corrupt by as high as 78.6 percent of the respondents interviewed. That the spirited campaign by the AAP raising the critical issues, as mentioned earlier, did count as the data showed that a significant 28.6 percent of the respondents made up their mind about their electoral choice only during the campaign.

CSDS-Lokniti post-poll survey data suggested that AAP gained electorally by presenting itself as a viable alternative in a state where, due to a stable bi-polar party system in place for a long time and the inability of any other party to remain relevant, electorates were not able to find alternative electoral choices even as they had become wary of the lacklustre performance of the successive Congress and the SAD-BJP governments. The electorates' dissatisfaction with the performance of both Congress-led UPA government at the centre and the SAD-BJP government in the state, as the survey data revealed, helped AAP to reap electoral dividend.

The success of AAP showed that a party could win elections in the state without resorting to money and muscle power and that elections in the state did not need to be 'managed'. As the subsequent developments have shown, AAP, a party in the making then, has not been able to maintain its momentum, as was hoped at that time.

2019 elections

Punjab 'exceptionalism', mentioned in the second chapter in the context of the electoral trend, was very much in evidence in the 2019 Lok Sabha elections as it was the only state in north India where the BJP in alliance with the SAD could not have an upper hand over the Congress. The verdict was almost a repeat of the 2014 Parliamentary elections. The electoral setback of the SAD-BJP alliance, was especially glaring as neighbouring state of Haryana and lower Himachal Pradesh region which were part of the greater Punjab voted overwhelmingly for the BJP. In fact, along with Kerala, Punjab was the only state in the entire country where the Congress registered impressive victories.

The narrative of national security, popularised by the BJP to its advantage after the Pulwama incident in insurgency afflicted Kashmir valley could not receive much traction among the electorates. Arguably, it was because electorates in the state in general and especially the ones residing in the border regions and engaged in cultivation and trade across the border have always suffered whenever there has been a war or even tension at the border. This explains why Punjabi voters, despite having a large presence in the armed forces and having wounded memories of the bloodied partition, still have been great votaries of peace on the border unlike the strong 'anti-Pakistan' feeling across India creating a short-term war-like hysteria and radical nationalism fuelled by religiosity. Then again, like in the 2014 elections, the state did not witness much of an impact of the 'Modi wave' that swept much of the Hindi heartland. This was despite the fact that SAD, a regionalist party always setting the electoral agenda on behalf of the SAD-BJP alliance in the past, this time tried to piggyback on the popularity of Narendra Modi making him the face of the SAD-BJP campaign and borrowing the BJP narrative of 'one nation, strong nation' under 'Modi Sarkar'.

As per the Lokniti post-poll survey, only three of every ten respondents interviewed preferred Narendra Modi as the next Prime Minister. This was much lower than the national support that Modi received for second-term Prime Ministership (47%). Underlining the regional specificity of this Sikh majority 'Punjabi Suba', if leadership factor mattered in influencing the electoral choices then it was once again (like in the 2017 Assembly elections) the leadership of the Congress Chief Minister Captain Amarinder Singh that mattered, projecting him as the undisputed leader of the Congress, reminding one of the Congress satrap of the Nehruvian days. It was he and not Rahul Gandhi who was the face of the Congress campaign. Since 2017 electoral success, Captain's position within the party has remained unchallenged barring the dissenting voices raised by his erstwhile cabinet colleague Navjot Singh Sidhu and former state unit president Pratap Singh Bajwa, both of whom have accused not doing enough on drug issue.

For any discernible observer of Punjab elections, this seemed a lacklustre election. Going by the lack of intensity during the campaign and participation in the election meetings coupled with the reported reluctance of the leaders to even contest despite being offered the tickets (especially in case of the SAD) was indicative of the lukewarm response of parties, leaders and voters to the election. The overall apathy was also reflected in the voters' relatively low turnout as the state is known for its higher turnout. As compared to the national voting average, Punjab was a percentage point lower. Further, it was close to four percentage points lower than the turnout recorded in the 2014 Lok Sabha polls. It clearly showed a lack of overall interest in the electoral contest. It was as if the main contestant parties like the election analysts/ pollsters seemed to know the final outcome well in advance even before entering into the fray. One can also add here that the three main contestant parties seemed happy to note the restoration of the old order with the SAD-BJP and the Congress once again forming two poles of a bipolar party system. As expected, Congress gained in this election by winning eight seats and four seats went to the SAD-BJP. Congress received 40 percent of the votes polled whereas the SAD-BJP alliance received 37 percent of the votes polled thereby losing two seats from the 2014 tally (Sekhon and Kumar, 2019).

As per the Lokniti survey data, Congress party led in all age groups of the voters as also among both men and women. Unlike in 2014 when the AAP was the most preferred party of the educated and highly educated, in 2019 it was the Congress. Congress also remained the first choice of all economic classes, i.e. poor, lower, middle, and rich. But, the highest percentage (42 percent) of the voters in its favour came from the rich class.

AAP could secure a lone victory in the form of Bhagwant Mann, the party state unit chief and sitting member from Sangrur. Mann's success could be credited more to his personal charisma/oratory and remaining in constant touch with his constituency than to his party affiliation (*The Tribune*, 16 May, 2019). AAP had received 24 percent of the vote polled and won four out of 13 Lok Sabha seats in 2014 and had repeated its success by emerging as the main opposition party in the 2017 Assembly elections, winning as many as 20 seats and polling at 24 percent of the vote. This time it got only seven percent of votes polled. Endemic factionalism, organisational weaknesses, centralised role of high command, absence of autonomy to the state leadership, ideological bankruptcy, among other factors, have seemingly put the AAP on the path to oblivion in the state even though the people in the state still yearn for a winnable third alternative. AAP leadership at Delhi, realising the party's vulnerable position, even had made an attempt to have alliance with the Congress, an offer rejected by state unit. AAP's loss of support benefitted the Congress as one fourth of those who had voted for the AAP last time, voted in this election for the Congress, as per the Lokniti post-poll survey data. The decline in terms of support helped the BJP-SAD alliance in the urban constituencies. The victory of BJP in Hindu-majority Gurdaspur and Hoshiarpur constituencies testified to it.

The BJP regained the Gurdaspur seat after its candidate had lost it to Congress candidate Sunil Jakhar, then state unit president, with a huge margin of more than 1.93 lakh votes in the by-poll in 2017. This time there was a massive shift of more than 2.70 lakh votes in the 2019 election. The BJP candidate Sunny Deol took a lead in seven out of nine Hindu dominated assembly constituencies. It was in this constituency sharing boundary with BJP dominated Jammu region and also Pakistan where the narrative of national security had an electoral impact. What also helped Deol, son of popular star of yesteryears Dharmendra, a self-proclaimed *Punjab da puttar*, was his own popular image built upon playing patriotic roles in the movies promoting jingoist nationalism (Sekhon and Kumar, 2019).

The results of these elections, however, showed that there is still a possibility of a viable third alternative in the future as the splinter parties (breakaway factions of AAP and SAD) forming people's democratic alliance (PDA) secured more than 2 percent of the votes polled, particularly in the rural areas—the traditional stronghold of Akalis. Simarjit Singh Bains, the candidate of PDA came second in Ludhiana constituency securing close to 30 percent of the votes. The PDA candidate from BSP took the lead in two assembly constituencies, i.e. Banga and Adampur in Jalandhar parliamentary seat. The vote share of PDA alliance was more than 10 percent of the total votes in these elections. This alliance consisted of six parties including Lok Insaf party, BSP, Punjab Ekta Party led by Sukhpal Singh Khaira who left the AAP just before the election, Punjab Ekta Party led by Dharamvir Gandhi, the sitting MP from Patiala, and two communist parties (Sekhon and Kumar, 2019).

SAD, as aforementioned, seemed resigned to its dismal fate and so the Badal family–led party devoted all its energy and resources to win the seats of Firozepur and Bathinda from where Sukhbir Badal and Harsimrat Badal contested. Even in these constituencies, Parkash Singh Badal despite his advanced age had to come out of his semi-retirement to campaign to ensure their victories. Even then Harsimrat Kaur could barely scrape through against young Congress candidate Amrinder Singh Raja Warring by a thin margin of 21,772 votes. Sukhbir Badal won from Ferozepur, which since 1985 has always voted for the SAD. The Akali defeats reflected poorly on the leadership of Sukhbir Badal, who has been the party president for a long time and was until recently virtually running the SAD-BJP state government as the deputy chief minister. The SAD has steadily been losing its core constituency of rural Sikhs as from once being a cadre based/ideologically rooted party known for dharma yudh morchas for the panthic and state's cause, it has become a 'family/dynastic party' that is seen as responsible for destroying the autonomy of the Akal Takht and SGPC, the other two vital institutions of Sikh politics. SAD leadership had to also take the blame for the ten years of misrule (2007–2017), which destroyed the economy of the state and brought rampant corruption in high places and drugs and mining mafia to the fore. Akali leadership also faced the people's wrath because of its leadership indulging in cultivating the controversial Dera Sacha Sauda chief for the Dera supporters' vote. Also what caused the loss of electoral support for the SAD was the SAD-BJP government failure to bring to justice the culprits of desecration of the Holy Sikh scripture and subsequent firing over the agitating masses in 2015 in Behbal Kalan that had followed the large-scale farmers' suicides due to cotton crops failure in Malwa region which was again blamed on the spurious pesticides supplied to the farmers in connivance of the government officials and leaders in power. Congress government used Justice Ranjit Singh Commission of Inquiry Report which after probing into incidents of desecration indicted Parkash Singh Badal being 'in the loop' about the decision to use force on the protesters. This was one factor that enabled the Congress candidate Jasbir Singh Dimpa to wrest the 'panthic seat' like Khadoor Sahib which since 1991 was with the SAD, defeating senior SAD leader Bibi Jagir Kaur.

The survey data showed that a majority of the voters interviewed considered the desecration issue as being very important. In addition, more than one third of the respondents considered police firing in Kotakpura as an important issue. Four of every ten Sikh respondents interviewed during the survey opined that the SAD could not uphold the honour of the Sikh faith whereas one fourth Sikhs interviewed somewhat agreed that the SAD disregarded the faith. Only one of every ten Sikh voters interviewed fully disagreed that SAD disregarded their faith. Akali's loss of its core social constituency helped the Congress as the post poll survey data showed that two out of five (37 percent) Jat Sikhs voted for the Congress which was 14 percentage point higher than in 2014 Lok Sabha election as per the Lokniti poll data. Survey revealed that the Congress managed to attract close to 18 percent of the voters support in this election who had voted for the SAD-BJP alliance in 2014 Lok Sabha election. The decline of the SAD meant that it was the BJP leaders and their agenda that defined the campaign of the two parties and also put a question mark over the longevity of the SAD-BJP alliance in the future. This is a distinct possibility as Punjab is a state where the party has failed to broaden its traditional urban support base, raise a state level leader, and emerge as winnable party on its own. In Punjab, it has been confined to 3 and 23 seats in Lok Sabha and Vidhan Sabha, respectively, and the Akalis have never allowed BJP to swap/increase its share of seats. But in this election, the biggest gainer in the alliance was the BJP, which could win two out of three seats it contested. As the survey showed, the SAD-BJP alliance received overwhelming support of the Hindu upper castes (58 percent), the credit for which would obviously go to the BJP. The BJP nationwide success and its failure to persuade SAD to allow it to contest on more seats both in the Lok Sabha and Assembly elections put a question mark over the longevity of the alliance (Sekhon and Kumar, 2019).

Finally, it was an election where the same electoral issues, namely the farmers' distress, drug menace, lack of jobs, large-scale migration of youth to the western countries, industries shifting to neighbourly states, corruption,

Table 6.1 Performance of Political Parties from 1996 Onward: Lok Sabha Elections in Punjab

Party name	Year of Lok Sabha Elections																				
	1996			1998			1999			2004			2009			2014			2019		
	Seats Contested	Won	Votes Polled	Seats Contested	Won	Votes Polled	Seats Contested	Won	Votes Polled	Seats Contested	Won	Votes Polled	Seats Contested	Won	Votes Polled	Seats Contested	Won	Votes Polled	Seats Contested	Won	Votes Polled
BSP	4	3	9.35%	4	0	12.65%	3	0	3.84%	13	0	7.67%	13	0	5.75%	13	0	1.91%	3	0	3.5%
CPI	3	0	1.60%	1	0	3.40%	1	1	3.74%	1	0	3.74%	2	0	0.33%	5	0	0.4%			
CPM	3	0	2.68%	3	0	1.06%	1	0	2.18%	1	0	2.18%	1	0	0.14%	3	0	0.13%			
INC	13	2	35.10%	8	0	25.85%	11	8	38.44%	11	2	34.17%	13	8	45.23%	13	3	33.19%	13	8	40.1%
SAD	9	8	28.72%	8	8	32.93%	9	2	28.59%	10	8	34.28%	10	4	33.85%	10	4	26.37%	10	2	27.45%
SAD(M)	7	0	3.85%	4	0	2.73%	1	1	3.41%	6	0	3.79%	3	0	0.36%						
IND	181	0	7.51%	49	1	4.91%	57	0	2.45%	70	0	2.75%	114	0	2.33%	118	0	3.61%	13	1	7.4%
AAP																13	4	24.47%			
BJP	13	0	6.48%	3	3	11.67%	3	1	9.16%	3	3	10.48%	3	1	10.06%	3	1	8.70%	3	2	9.63%

Source: CSDS data unit.

depleting water table, and education were raised by the parties, hardly receiving enthusiastic responses, unlike 2014 and 2017 when, thanks to the AAP campaign, drug abuse and corruption in high places were major issues. The fact of the matter is that the parties in power have invariably failed to address any of these issues. So it is basically a victory of the Congress by default as there is an absence of a viable third alternative and loss of credibility to the SAD.

Notes

1 However, despite SAD affirming its alliance with BJP in Chandigarh constituency also, there was hardly any Akali support for BJP candidate Satyapal Jain. G.S. Riar, the city unit president of SAD, openly supported INLD candidate Harmohan Dhawan. It did contribute to the victory of Congress candidate Pawan Bansal who trounced his archrival by a margin of 45,248 votes securing 52 percent of the votes. Interestingly whereas Congress lost 4 percent of the votes in 2004 election as compared to 1999 in Punjab, it gained by 5 percent in Chandigarh.

2 Total number of voters in Punjab was 1, 68, 80, 412 comprising of 87, 86, 543 men and 80, 93, 869 women.

3 The vote share of the Congress candidate Pawan Bansal in 2004 and 2009 election for Chandigarh constituency was 52 percent and 47 percent, respectively, which was much higher than the BJP candidate Satyapal Jain vote share of 35 and 30 percent.

4 The party merged with the Akali Dal on the eve of the 2012 Assembly elections.

5 Apprehension had been raised by the Congress about the possibility of violence and malpractices in the elections on the basis of the unprecedented violence witnessed in the local bodies elections held in the summer of 2008.

6 The party merged with SAD on the eve of the 2012 Assembly elections.

7 Apprehension had been raised by the Congress about the possibility of violence and malpractices in the elections on the basis of the unprecedented violence witnessed in the local bodies elections held in 2008 summer.

8 The number of assembly constituencies reserved for SC increased from 29 to 34 in the 2009 delimitation exercise.

9 In the 2007 Assembly elections, the Congress won 44 of the 117 seats, most of the victories recorded in the Malwa region, traditionally considered the Akali bastion. Congress won in 37 out of 67 seats from Malwa region. The SAD-BJP combine, reminiscent of the 1997 elections, won 20 out of 25 seats in the Doaba region and 23 out of 27 seats in the Majha region.

10 In the 2012 Assembly elections also Dera Sacha Sauda had avoided issuing any specific directive to its followers in favour of any party. Candidates from Congress and SAD, however, did meet the Dera Chief seeking his support.

11 As per the Election Commission data, SAD received on an average a vote share of 31 percent in the nine Assembly elections since the 1967 elections as compared to Congress average vote share of 38 percent in the last ten Assembly elections held during the same period. The average figure for the SAD in the last 11 Lok Sabha elections till 2009 was 31 percent whereas the Congress received on an average 38 percent of votes polled in the last 12 Lok Sabha elections. Thus, given their limited social support base, it has been a compulsion for SAD to have an electoral alliance with BJP.

12 Even in the post-poll survey conducted after 2012 Assembly elections which saw Sukhbir Badal emerging as the chief architect of SAD-BJP victory, only 5 percent of the respondents preferred him as chief minister compared to 38 percent in favour of Badal senior and 33 percent for Amarinder Singh.

13 What goes in favour of Parkash Singh Badal is his popular image of being a moderate Akali who has been a 'reconciler' in a state where the Hindu-Sikh relations witnessed strain during the days of militancy.

14 In 2012, Assembly elections SAD gave tickets to as many 11 Hindu candidates out of which 10 won.

15 When asked during the survey whether they agreed or disagreed with the statement—instead of Chandigarh, some other city of the state should be made the capital of Punjab, only 10 percent of the respondents as against 48 percent of the respondents agreed with the statement.

16 One of the most important factors in explaining the verdict in favour of SAD-BJP government was the direct transfer of public resources to the masses under anti-poverty schemes like providing subsidised flour and lentils, distribution of cycles to the girl students, and monetary benefits to the parents of marriageable girls. Massive subsidies in the form of free power and water to the farmers continued. It is not that the Congress did not promise to continue it all but that the electorates had greater faith in their commitment (read audacity) to continue the schemes irrespective of the precarious state of treasury.

17 The successive state governments in the state unfailingly put forward three oft-repeated 'explanations' for the economic predicament that the state finds itself in while absolving themselves from the charges of economic mismanagement. The argument goes like this: first, the state has paid a heavy economic price on account of its more than a decade-old fight against militancy as it became debt ridden as a result; second, investments that dried up during the conflict period have not picked up to this day as the neighbouring hill states have been doling out incentives to the potential investors as they enjoy special category status; third, the debts have also accumulated due to the heavy subsidies being given to the farmers who in turn have contributed to the nation's cause by replenishing its food grains stocks for ensuring food security.

18 39 percent of the 3,250 respondents interviewed in Lokniti survey were of the opinion that SAD-BJP government performed better than the preceding Congress government. More decisively 54 per cent of farmers thought that their condition had improved during the SAD-BJP regime.

19 This part draws extensively from Kumar (2014a).

20 In terms of electoral participation, Punjab has been consistently registering higher than national average. In 2014, for a total of 13 parliamentary seats in Punjab electoral roll had listed 1, 90, 8008 voters out of which 13,845,132 actually voted. There were 266 candidates in the fray including 118 independent candidates. Voter turnout was 70.6 percent, which was higher than 69.7 percent votes polled in the 2009 parliamentary elections. Signify the importance of 'local', electoral participation in the state has been higher in the assembly elations in comparison to the parliamentary elections.

21 To the credit of the new party, it drew over 10 million voters towards it though they remained spatially dispersed to the disadvantage of the party under the first past-the-post system (Wyatt b, 2015, p. 10).

22 However, BJP vote share in all these non-Hindi speaking states also went up. In Jammu and Kashmir, Assam, and West Bengal the increase was particularly significant.

23 Electoral success in neighbouring Haryana was expected because of three factors: first, the 'satellite' effect of neighbouring Delhi; second, the campaign of the AAP that veered around fighting the corruption in high places found resonance in the state reeling under the corrupt practices of land mafia; third, Arvind Kejriwal, the top party leader, belonging to the state (Kumar, 2014b). As it turned out, the party was routed both in Delhi and Haryana just like elsewhere, though it did manage to get a significant number of votes in Delhi keeping its hope alive for a comeback, a hope that was fulfilled in the 2014 winter assembly elections

24 Learning a lesson from the results, AAP leadership decided to concentrate all its energy and resources to face the Assembly elections in Delhi and they succeeded in sweeping the elections by leaving only three seats for the BJP in a 70-seat state assembly.

25 Some of these sates were Odisha, Tamil Nadu, Karnataka, Kerala, Assam, Andhra Pradesh, Telangana and West Bengal, Jammu and Kashmir, among others.

26 Though given the organisational weakness and the absence of a state-level leader in the state, it would be probably unrealistic on the part of the BJP to imagine itself in a position to fight elections alone in near future like it did in neighbouring Haryana in 2014 Assembly elections.

27 Lokniti survey data showed that the percentage of the respondents between the ages of 18 and 25 who voted for the AAP was highest among all the parties in the fray.

28 When asked while making their electoral choice whether they gave importance to the local candidate or to the state-level leadership of the party or to the Prime Ministerial candidate, 23.9 percent of the respondents said it was the local candidate and 26.8 percent said it was the Prime Ministerial candidate.

29 Taking a clue from the AAP success in 2014, Amarinder Singh raised the drug issue in a big way during his campaign, squarely blaming Akali politicians including Badal junior's brother-in-law Bikram Singh Majithia.

7 Conclusion
Looking ahead

Sifting through the election studies in India in the last three decades, one can discern some common emergent trends, which are visible in most of the states even as exceptionalism also get highlighted in state-specific analysis. As discussed in the preceding chapters, most states have witnessed the emergence of state-level parties in a big way in the last three decades coinciding with the decline of the Congress. Along with state parties, state-level political leadership across the party lines have also risen, having a distinct national impact. In another commonality, India's party system has also moved towards electoral bipolarity or two-party system in most of the states despite the overall fragmentation of party system. In addition, states have also been witness to the emergence of distinct electoral regions as politicisation and mobilisation takes place along the regional/sub-regional lines. As a consequence of these developments, there has been an ascendance of local/state-specific issues rather than the national issues in the elections, especially at the state level. These trends have held even as BJP has emerged as the dominant/system-defining party. Though the future of small/minor parties looks bleak, larger state parties with their own strong regional identities are likely to linger on.

Punjab shares the aforementioned electoral trends with other states as is clear from discussion in the preceding chapters. For a long time, the state has witnessed the emergence of its historical-cultural regions turning into distinct political/electoral regions. Also Akali Dal, a state-level party has been shaping the political/electoral agenda of the state for a long time.[1] Despite recent electoral setbacks, the ethnic/regionalist party, identified with the making of Punjabi Suba and its unresolved issues, continues to remain electorally relevant. The challenge before the party as of now, however, is to retain its organisational presence. The rise of Badal senior as the undisputed party leader ensured unity within the usually factions-ridden party in to last two decades. But his colossal leadership has also turned the once cadre-based party into a 'family party' in a literal sense. The dominance of Badal family in the party has also witnessed the decimation of the other two historically autonomous Sikh institutions i.e. Akal Takht and SGPC. The organisational and ideological decline of the party that commenced in the days of militancy and continued unabated even after under the watch of Badal has alienated the traditional supporters of the party. The party of late also faces the leadership issue. Despite remaining the party president and deputy chief minister for more than a decade, Sukhbir Badal as 'inheritor' is yet to acquire the state-wide support base as a leader in his own right. Another challenge for the SAD has been to expand its support base beyond the Jat Sikhs, which has also become shaky due to the party being seen as wavering from its stated ideals. As discussed in the preceding chapters, the social base of the SAD has historically remained in sharp contrast to that of the Congress. While the Congress continues to receive the support from both Hindus and Sikhs and also from rural as well as urban segments, SAD contesting on its own is likely to get electoral support from only a small segment of the Hindus of the state. In addition, even among the Sikhs, as discussed previously, it fails to attract the backward castes and the Scheduled castes. In other words, SAD continues to be perceived as the party of Jat Sikhs and Khatris though the party has been able to get the votes from other communities also. While most of the states in India have been witness to the vociferous articulation of the aspirations of the lower castes, how far can the Akali Dal manage to ignore these aspirations is a moot question, given the predominantly Jat Sikh leadership in the party. If it continues to do that, then factionalism and decline is bound to afflict it as was already reflected in the 2019 elections.

Given the fact that any coalitional arrangement is always the second best choice to capture political power for any political party, it is imperative that SAD has been trying to widen its social support base in the state. This would be very much more applicable to an ascendant BJP as it would strengthen the party's bargaining position vis-à-vis Akalis. The electoral strategy of the BJP regarding the states where the party had to start from scratch has been to enter into alliance as a junior partner with the local state party, pitted against the Congress and then build and expand its support base to emerge finally as a winnable party. Punjab has so far been an exception and so the desire of the party state leadership is natural. With the growing clout of the party nationwide and demand of the state unit since 2014, the party state unit has been asking for a greater seat share and also to be allowed to swap the seats under the existing coalitional arrangement. In fact after the two successive Lok Sabha victories and wins in the Assembly elections, the disgruntled voices have arisen from the ranks. The BJP central leadership, however, has so far desisted to take any step. This can be explained in the party's inability to throw up a party leader having state-wide support. The party also does not have much organisational presence in rural Punjab nor has it been able to get support of the rural Sikh community. Also there has been a lurking danger that the split in the SAD-Akali combine vote would actually go a long way in helping the rival Congress, making it almost invincible.

As discussed in the preceding chapters, despite having very high voter turnouts and closely contested elections accompanied by electoral volatility, the social basis of political power in the state has been too narrow. The state has a sizable number of Scheduled castes. They constitute one-third of the state's population. Their politicisation and mobilisation, however, is still an unfinished task unlike the neighbouring states of north India. BSP after tasting initial electoral success has declined irreversibly and now has some limited presence only in Doaba region. The party has been hit by endemic factionalism and neglect of the party national leader. The Scheduled castes community is not effectively represented in the leadership role in any other party either despite 34 out of 117 seats being reserved for them in the assembly. The narrow basis of political power is reflected in the way parties vie with each other to get the support of flourishing Deras and the religious sects' heads and through them get the dalit votes.

Arguably, entrenched bi-polarity and narrow social basis of political power has not helped in ensuring the economic well-being of the state that has been too much dependent on farming. The Green Revolution has already run its course long back which in any case benefitted the large landholding farmers that too in the short run. As a result of uncontrolled use of ground water and fertilisers in a capital driven agrarian sector, long-term crisis has engulfed the state with even the landowning farmers committing suicides. Successive governments bent upon indulging in reckless populism have failed to address the issue despite repeated assurance to diversify the economy by reviving the once famed manufacturing sectors of the state besides developing the agro-based industries. Instead of taking corrective measures, the political leadership continues to blame the landlocked boundaries of the state, it being the borderland state as well as blaming the centre for giving incentives to the neighbouring states that have caused the state-based industries to shift.

Endemic economic crisis, lack of effective governance, and institutionalised corruption are among the factors that have caused the state electorates to look for a viable third alternative. The rise of AAP in 2014 gave a glimpse of hope to the electorates. For a brief period of time, there was a three-party system in the state. However, as discussed in the preceding chapter, the party of late has been in serious trouble due to incessant infighting, defections, and excessive control by Delhi-based non-Punjabi leadership. As for the smaller parties/breakaway groups 'coming together' to contest elections every time they take place, be it for the Lok Sabha or Assembly, they have never succeeded in winning the seats under the first past the post electoral system. The 2019 Lok Sabha election verdict was an election when the smaller parties' alliance got an impressive vote share but no seats.

While referring to mainstream parties' manifestos, and campaigns in the successive elections held after 1997 in the state, be it for the assembly or the Lok Sabha, it becomes clear that there has been a paradigmatic shift in the state electoral politics from 'religious-political' issues to 'political-economic' issues, i.e. issues of 'performance', 'development', and 'governance'. This is particularly true for the SAD, a panthic party that has played the role of catalyst in the state politics. There has been convergence of electoral agenda in the sense that all the mainstream parties have been seeking vote in the name of the Hindu-Sikh unity, communal peace and harmony, and in the name of development. This situation has not changed even as religion of late has become such a major factor in influencing the electoral choices in recent India.

It is imperative that the established parties' leadership in the state make conscious efforts to institutionalize their party organs and democratise party institutional set up to curb the emerging personalising and centralising mode of politics that characterise the state politics. Parties depending heavily on patronage and 'social engineering' without much care for democratic ethos or public ethics does not help. The lopsidedness/degeneration of polity and parties' leadership overdependence on populism/clientelism impact adversely on any effort to go for much needed substantive public policies initiatives.

Note

1 SAD for a long time has continued to 'articulate aspirations of Punjabi regional nationalism along with trying to protect the interests of the Sikhs as a religious minority in India and abroad . . . (being) second oldest (next only to Congress) political party in Punjab, and the oldest regional party in India . . . (it) views various politico-economic issues from the perspective of their impact and implications for Punjab' (Singh, Pritam, 2014).

References

Ahsan, Aitzaz and Meghnad Desai. 2005. *Divided By Democracy*. Delhi: Roly Books.

Akbar, M. J. 1985. *India: The Siege Within*. London: Harmondsworth.

Alam, Javeed. 1986. 'Political Implications of Economic Contradictions in Punjab', *Social Scientist*, 14(10): 3–26.

Anand, J. C. 1976. 'Punjab: Politics of Retreating Communalism', in Iqbal Narain (ed.), *State Politics in India*. New Delhi: Meenakshi Prakashan.

Ayyangar, S. and Suraj Jacob. 2014. 'Question Hour Activity and Party Behaviour in India', *The Journal of Legislative Studies*, 21(2): 232–49.

Baixas, Lionel. 2007. 'The Dera Sacha Sauda Controversy and Beyond', *Economic and Political Weekly*, XLII(40): 4059–65.

Bajwa, Harcharan Singh. 1979. *Fifty Years of Punjab Politics (1920–1970)*. Chandigarh: Modem Publishers.

Brass, Paul R. 1965. *Factional Politics in an Indian State: The Congress Party in Uttar Pradesh*. Berkeley: University of California Press.

Brass, Paul R. 1974. *Language, Religion and Politics in North India*. Cambridge: Cambridge University Press.

Burns, James M. 1978. *Leadership*. New York: Harper and Row.

Chandhoke, Neera and Praveen Priyadarshi. 2006. 'Electoral Politics in Post-Conflict Societies: Case of Punjab', *EPW*, March 4, www.epw.org.in/showarticles.

Chandra, Kanchan. 2004. *Why Ethnic Parties Succeed: Patronage and Ethnic Headcounts in India*. Cambridge: Cambridge University Press.

Chandra, Kanchan. 2012. 'Whither Identity Politics?', *Frontline*, March 28, www. frontlineonnet.com/stories/20120406290602100.htm (accessed on 23 April 2019).

Chandra, Kanchan. 2016. (ed.). *Democratic Dynasties: State, Party and Family in Contemporary Indian Politics*. Cambridge: Cambridge University Press.

Chhibber, Pradeep. 2013. 'Dynastic Parties: Organisation, Finance and Impact', *Party Politics*, 12(1): 277–95.

Chhibber, Pradeep and Geetha Murali. 2006. 'Duvergerian Dynamics in the Indian States', *Party Politics*, 12(2006): 5–34.

Chhibber, Pradeep and Rahul Verma. 2014. 'The BJP's 2014 "Modi Wave": An Ideological Consolidation of the Right', *Economic and Political Weekly*, XLIX(39): 50–6.

Church, Roderick. 1984. 'The Pattern of State Politics in Indira Gandhi's India', in John R. Wood (ed.), *State Politics in Contemporary India: Crisis or Continuity*. Boulder: West View Press.

Corsi, Marco. 2006. 'Communalism and the Green Revolution in Punjab', *Journal of Developing Societies*, 22(2): 85–109.

Das, Samir Kumar. 2009. 'Democracy's Janus Face: A Review of Elections in Post Independence India', in Sharmila Mitra Deb and M. Manisha (eds.), *Indian Democracy: Problems and Prospects*. Delhi: Anthem Press, pp. 90–106.

Deol, Harnik. 2000. *Religion and Nationalism in India: The Case of Punjab*. London: Routledge.

Dhami, S. S. 1981. 'Caste, Class and Politics in the Rural Punjab', in Paul Wallace and Surendra Chopra (eds.), *Political Dynamics of Punjab*. Amritsar: Guru Nanak Dev University Press.

Diwakar, Rekha. 2017. *Party System in India*. New Delhi: Oxford University Press.

Dyke, Virginia Van. 2009. 'The Khalistan Movement in Punjab, India, and the Post-Militancy Era', *Asian Survey*, 49(6): 975–97.

Farooqui, Adnan and E. Sridharan. 2016. 'Can Umbrella Parties Survive? The Decline of the Indian National Congress', *Commonwealth & Comparative Politics*, 54(3): 331–61.

Forrester, D. B. 1966. 'Changing Patterns of Political Leadership in India', *The Review of Politics*, 28(3): 308–18.

Gill, Mehar Singh. 2017. 'Demographic Dynamism of Punjab, 1971–2011', *Economic and Political Weekly*, LII(3): 26–9.

Grewal, J. S. 1996. *The Akalis: A Short History*. Chandigarh: Punjab Studies Publications.

Guha, Ramchandra. 2010. 'Political Leadership', in Niraja Gopal Jayal and Pratap Bhanu Mehta (eds.), *The Oxford Companion to Politics in India*. New Delhi: Oxford University Press.

Gulati, K. C. 1974. *The Akalis: Past and Present*. New Delhi: Ashajanak Publication.

Hopkin, Jonathan. 2019. 'Conceptualising Political Clientelism: Political exchange and Democratic Theory', Unpublished Paper, www.researchgate.net (accessed on 15 July 2019).

Jaffrelot, Christophe. 2003. *India's Silent Revolution: The Rise of Low Castes in North Indian Politics*. Delhi: Permanent Black.

Jaffrelot, Christophe. 2015. 'Explaining the 2014 Lok Sabha Elections: Introduction', *Studies in Indian Politics*, 27 May:151–166.

Jeffrey, Robin. 1987. 'Grappling with History: Sikh Politicians and the Past', *Pacific Affairs*, 60(1), Spring, 1987: 59–72.

Jeffrey, Robin. 1994. *What's Happening to India? Punjab, Ethnic Conflict and the Test for Federalism*. London: Macmillan.

Jodhka, Surinder, 1997, 'Crisis of the 1980s and changing agenda of punjab studies: A Survey of Some Recent Research', *Economic and Political Weekly*, 35(11), pp. 877–79.

Jodhka, Surinder. 2000a. 'Decline of Identity Politics', *Economic and Political Weekly*, 35(11): pp. 877–79.

Jodhka, Surinder S. 2000b. 'Prejudice Without Pollution? Scheduled Castes in Contemporary Punjab', *Journal of Indian School of Political Economy*, 12(3 & 4): 381–404.

Jodhka, Surinder S. 2000c. 'The Ravi Dasis of Punjab: Global Contours of Caste and Religious Strife', *Economic and Political Weekly*, 44(24): 79–85.

Jodhka, Surinder S. 2002. 'Caste and Untouchability in Rural Punjab', *Economic and Political Weekly* 38(19): 1813–23.

Jodhka, Surinder S. 2005. 'Return of the Region: Identities and Electoral Politics in Punjab', *Economic and Political Weekly*, XL(3): 224–30.

Judge, Paramjit Singh. 2012. 'Punjab Elections: Entrenching Akali Dominance', *Economic and Political Weekly*, XLVIL(18): 17–20.

Judge, Paramjit Singh and Gurpreet Bal. 2009. *Mapping Dalits: Contemporary Reality and Future Prospects in Punjab*. Jaipur: Rawat.

Kailash, K. K. 2014a. 'Regional Parties in the 16th Lok Sabha Elections: Who Survived and Why?', *Economic and Political Weekly*, XLIX(39): 64–71.

Kailash, K. K. 2014b. 'Institutionalising a Coalitional System and Games Within Coalitions in India (1996–2014)', *Studies in Indian Politics*, 2(2): 185–202.

Kalra, Virinder S. 2014. 'Secular and Religious (Miri/Piri) Domains in Sikhism', in Pashura Singh and Louis E. French (eds.), *The Oxford Handbook of Sikh Studies*. Oxford: Oxford University Press, pp. 262–70.

Kapur, R. A. 1986. *Sikh Separatism: The Politics of Faith*. London: Allen and Unwin.

Khilnani, Sunil. 1997. *The Idea of India*. London: Hamish Hamilton.

Kinnvall, Catarina. 2006. *Globalisation and Religious Nationalism in India: The Search for Ontological Security*. London: Routledge.

Kondo, Norio. 2007. 'Election Studies in India', Discussion paper No. 8, *Institute of Developing Economies*, JETRO, Chiba, pp. 1–18.

Kothari, Rajni. 1964. 'The Congress "System" in India', *Asian Survey*, 4(12): 1163–73.

Kumar, Ashutosh. 2003. 'State Electoral Politics: Looking for the Larger Picture', *Economic and Political Weekly*, July 26: 3145–7.

Kumar, Ashutosh. 2004a. 'Punjab: In Search of New Leadership', *Economic and Political Weekly*, December 18: 5441–4.

Kumar, Ashutosh. 2004b. 'Electoral Politics in Punjab: Study of Akali Dal', *Economic and Political Weekly*, XLIV (39), April 3–10: 1515–20.

Kumar, Ashutosh. 2007. 'Punjab Elections: Exploring the Verdict', *Economic and Political Weekly*, 42, June 2: 2043–7.

Kumar, Ashutosh. 2011. 'Electoral Politics in Indian States: Exploring the Trends', *Seminar*, 620, April: 77–83.

Kumar, Ashutosh. 2012a. '2012 Assembly Elections in Punjab: Ascendance of a State Level Party', *Journal of Punjab Studies*, 9(2), Fall: 255–74.

Kumar, Ashutosh. 2012b. 'Just Another Elections?', *Seminar*, 631, March.

Kumar, Ashutosh. 2014a. 'Deras as Sites of Electoral Mobilisation in Indian Punjab: Explaining Why Political Parties Do Flock to the Deras', *Asian Ethnicity*, 17(3), June: 335–50, Routledge, London.

Kumar, Ashutosh. 2014b. 'Parliamenary Elections in Punjab: Explaining the Electoral Success of Aam Aadmi Party', *Journal of Punjab Studies*, University of California, Santa Barbara, 21(1): 113–127.

Kumar, Ashutosh. 2017a. 'Electoral Politics in Indian Punjab: A New Phase?', *South Asia Research*, 37(1): 223–34, Sage, London.

Kumar, Ashutosh. 2017b. 'Moving Beyond Nation State: Framing State Level Politics in India', *India Review*, 16(3): 277–303, Routledge.

Kumar, Ashutosh. 2018. 'Electoral Politics in Punjab: A Study of Shiromani Akali Dal', *Japanese Journal of Political Science*, 19(1): 1–20, Cambridge University Press.

Kumar, Ashutosh. 2019a. 'Studying Elections and Electoral Politics in the Indian States: An Introduction', in Ashutosh Kumar and Yatindra Singh Sisodia (eds.), *How India Votes: A State-by-state Look*. Hyderabad: Orient Blackswan, pp. 1–37.

Kumar, Ashutosh. 2019b. 'The 2019 Lok Sabha Elections in Punjab: Explaining the Success of Aam Aadmi Party', in Ashutosh Kumar and Yatindra Singh Sisodia (eds.), *How India Votes: A State-by-state Look*. Hyderabad: Orient Blackswan, pp. 144–62.

Kumar, Ashutosh. 2019c. 'Political Leadership at State Level in India: Continuity and Change', *India Review*, 18(3): 264–87.

Kumar, Ashutosh and Hardeep Kaur. 2019. 'Sikh Politics in Punjab: Shiromani Akali Dal', in Narendra Kumar (ed.), *Politics and Religion in India*. New Delhi: Routledge (co-authored), pp. 43–63.

Kumar, Ashutosh, Khusboo Mahajan and Kuldeep Kaur. 2018. 'The 2017 Assembly Election in Punjab: Emergence of a Triangular Electoral System'. *Journal of Sikh and Punjab Studies*, 25(1): 105–120.

Kumar, Ashutosh and Sanjay Kumar. 2002. 'Punjab Assembly Elections: Decline of Identity Politics', *Economic and Political Weekly*, April 13.

Kumar, Ashutosh and Jagrup Singh Sekhon. 2009. 'Punjab: Resurgence of the Congress', *Economic and Political Weekly*, 44(39), September 26: 183–6.

Kumar, Ashutosh and Jagrup Singh Sekhon. 2014. 'Punjab: Towards Consolidation of a Bipolar polity', in Suhas Palshikar K. C. Suri, and Yogendra Yadav (eds.), *Party Competition in Indian States: Electoral Politics in Post-Congress Polity*. New Delhi: Oxford University Press.

Kumar, Ashutosh and T. R. Sharma. 2009a. 'Legislative Elite in Punjab: A Socio-political Study', in Christophe Jaffrelot and Sanjay Kumar (eds.), *Rise of the Plebeians? The Changing Face of Indian Legislative Assemblies*. New Delhi: Routledge.

Kumar, Pramod. 2014. 'Coalition Politics in Punjab; From Communal Polarisation in Catch-all Parties', in E. Sridharan (ed.), *Coalition Politics in India; Selected Issues at the Centre and the States*. New Delhi: Academic Foundation, pp. 219–316.

Kumar, Pramod. 2017. 'Punjab Politics: Contesting Identities and Forging Coalitions', *Economic and Political Weekly*, LII(3): 44–9.

Kumar, Sanjay and Pranav Gupta. 2015. 'Changing Patterns of Women's Turnout in Indian Elections', *Studies in Indian Politics*, 3(1): 7–18.

Lal, Madan. 2009. 'Gurudom: The Political Dimension of Religious Sects in the Punjab', *South Asia Research*, 29(3): 223–34.

Lama-Rewal, Stephanie Tawa. 2009. 'Studying Elections in India: Scientific and Political Debates', *South Asia Multidisciplinary Academic Journal* (SAMAJ), 3: 2, www.indiaenvironmentportal.org.in/files/file/elections%20inIndia.pdf (accessed on 12 March 2017).

Lamba, G. K. 1999. *Dynamics of Punjabi Suba Movement*. New Delhi; Deep and Deep Publication.

MacMillan, Alistair. 2010. 'The Election Commission' in *Oxford Companion to Indian Politics* (eds). Niraja Gopal Jayal and Pratap Bhanu Mehta, 98–116, New Delhi: Oxford University Press.

Malik, Yogenra K. 1986. 'The Akali Party and Sikh Militancy', *Asian Survey*, XXVI(3), March: 345–62.

Manor, James. 2010. 'Beyond Clientelism: Digvijay Singh's Participatory, Pro-Poor Strategy in Madhya Pradesh', in P. Price and A. E. Rudd (eds.), *Power and Influence in India: Bosses, Lords and Captains*. New Delhi: Routledge, pp. 193–213.

Mendelsohn, Oliver and Marika Vicziany. 2000. *The Untouchables: Subordination, Poverty and the State in Modern India*. New Delhi: Cambridge University Press.

Morris-Jones, W. H. 1964. *The Government and Politics of India*. London: Hutchinson University Library.

Narang, Amarjit Singh. 2014. 'The Shiromani Akali Dal', in Pasaura Singh and Louis E. French (eds.), *The Oxford Handbook of Sikh Studies*. Oxford: Oxford University Press, pp. 339–49.

Nayar, Baldev Raj. 1968. 'Punjab', in Myron Weiner (ed.), *State Politics in India*. Princeton: Princeton University Press.

Nesbitt, Eleanor. 2010. *Sikhism: A Very Short Introduction*. New Delhi: Oxford University Press.

Nikolenyi, Casaba. 2010. *Minority Governments in India: The Puzzle of Elusive Majorities*. London and New York: Routledge.

Oberoi, Harjot. 1994. *The Construction of Religious Boundaries: Culture, Identity and Diversity in the Sikh Tradition*. Delhi: Oxford University Press.

Palshikar, Suhas and K. C. Suri. 2014. 'India's 2014 Lok Sabha Elections: Critical Shifts in the Long Term, Caution in the Short Term', *Economic and Political Weekly*, XLIX(39): 39–49.

Palshikar, Suhas. 2017. *Indian Democracy*. New Delhi: Oxford University Press.

Pettigrew, J. J. M. 1995. *The Sikhs of the Punjab: Unheard Voices of State and Guerrilla Violence*. London and NJ: Zed Books.

Purewal, Shinder. 2000. *Sikh Ethnonationalism and the Political Economy of Punjab*. New Delhi: Oxford University Press.

Puri, Harish. 1995. 'Akali Politics: Emerging Compulsions', in Virendra Grover (ed.), *The Story of Punjab: Yesterday and Today*. New Delhi: Deep and Deep Publications.

Ram, Ronki. 2004. 'Untochability in India with a difference: Ad Dharm, Dalit Assertion and Conflicts in Punjab, *Asian Survey*, 44, November-December, pp. 895–910.

Ram, Ronki. 2012. 'Beyond Conversion and Sanskritisation: Articulating an Alternative Dalit Agenda in East Punjab', *Modern Asian Studies*, 46(3): 639–702.

Ram, Ronki. 2017. 'Internal Caste Cleavages Among Dalits in Punjab', *Economic and Political Weekly*, LII(3): 54–7.

Roy, Ramashray and Paul Wallace (eds.). 1999. *Indian Politics and the 1998 Elections: Regionalism, Hindutva and State Politics*. New Delhi: Sage.

Rudolph, Susanne Hoeber and Lloyd I. Rudolph. 2008. 'Congress Learns to Lose: From a One-Party Dominant to a Multiparty System in India', in Edward Friedman and Joseph Wong (eds.), *Political Transitions in Dominant Party Systems: Learning to Lose*. London: Routledge.

Sardesai, Shreyas and Jyoti Mishra. 2017. 'Time of Vote Choice in India', *Studies in Indian Politics*, 5(1): 82–91.

Sarhadi, Ajit Singh. 1970. *Punjabi Suba: The Story of the Struggle*. Delhi: UB Kapoor and Sons.

Sekhon, Jagrup Singh and Ashutosh Kumar. 2019. 'An Outlier in the North: Success of the Congress in Punjab', *Economic and Political Weekly*, LIV(33), August 21: 10–12.

Sharma, T. R. 1986. 'Diffusion and Accommodation: The Contending Strategies of the Congress Party and Akali Dal in Punjab', Pacific *Affairs*, 59(4): 634–54.

Shastri, Sandeep, K. C. Suri and Yogendra Yadav (eds.). 2009. *Electoral Politics in Indian States. Lok Sabha Elections in 2004 and Beyond*. New Delhi: Oxford University Press.

Singh, Ajit. 2005. *Shiromani Akali Dal Religio-Political Study (1947–90)*. Kapurthala: Armann Publications.

Singh, Dalip. 1978. 'Sixth Lok Sabha Elections in Punjab: A New Dimension in State Politics', *The Indian Journal of Political Science*, 39(2): 210–27, www.jstor.org/stable/41854842/ (accessed on 24 September 2018).

Singh, Dalip. 1981. *Dynamics of Punjab Politics*. New Delhi: Macmillan India.

Singh, Gurharpal. 1997. 'The Akalis and the BJP in Punjab: From Ayodhya to the 1997 Legislative Assembly Election', in Thomas Blom Hansen and Christopher Jaffrelot (eds.), *The BJP and the Compulsions of Politics in India*. Delhi: Oxford University Press.

Singh, Khuswant. 1977. *A History of Sikhs*. Vol II. Delhi: Oxford University Press.

Singh, Mohinder. 1988. *The Akali Struggle*. New Delhi: Atlantic Publishers.

Singh, Manjit. 2012. 'A Re-election in Punjab and the Continuing Crisis', *Economic and Political Weekly*, XLVIL (13): 21–23.

Singh, Nirmal. 2014. 'BSP in Punjab: Analysing Its Failure', *Economic and Political Weekly*, 49(48): 17–19.

Singh, Pritam. 2007a. 'Punjab's Electoral Competition', *Economic and Political Weekly*, XLII(6), February 10: 466–7.

Singh, Pritam. 2007b. 'The Political Economy of the Cycles of Violence and Non-violence in the Sikh Struggle for Identity and Political Power: Implications for Indian federalism', *Third World Quarterly*, 28(3): 555–70.

Singh, Pritam. 2014. 'Class, Nation and Religion: Changing Nature of Akali Dal Politics in Punjab, India', *Commonwealth & Comparative Politics*, 52(1): 55–77.

Sirsikar, V. M.1965. 'Political Leadership in India', *Economic and Political Weekly*, 17(12), 20 March, 1965:517–522.

Sisson, Richard. 1972. *The Congress Party in Rajasthan: Political Integration and Institution Building in an Indian State*. Berkeley: University of California Press.

Sondhi, Aditya. 2016. 'Elections', in Sujit Choudhry, Madhav Khosla and Pratap Bhanu Mehta (eds.), *The Oxford Handbook of the Indian Constitution*. New Delhi: Oxford University Press.

Sridharan, E. 2012. 'Why Are Multi-party Minority Governments Viable in India? Theory and Comparison', *Commonwealth and Comparative Politics*, 50(3): 314–43.

Sridharan, E. 2014. 'Why Are Multi-Party Minority Governments Viable in India? Theory and comparison', in E Sridharan (ed.), *Coalition Politics in India : Selected Issues at the Centre and the States*. New Delhi: Academic Foundation, pp. 35–70.

Sridharan, E. and Milan Vaishnav. 2016. 'India', in Pippa Norris and Andrea Abel van (eds.), *Check Book Elections? Political Finance in Comparative Perspective*. New York: Oxford University Press.

Stern, Robert W. 2001. *Democracy and Dictatorship in South Asia: Dominant Classes and Political Outcomes in India, Pakistan and Bangladesh*. Westport: Praeger.

Talbot, A. 1980. 'The 1946 Punjab Elections', *Modern Asian Studies*, 14(1): 65–91.

Talbot, A. 2007. 'The Punjab Under Colonialism: Order and Transformation in British India', *Journal of Punjab Studies*, 14(1): 1–10.

Tanwar, Raghuvendra. 1999. *Politics of Sharing Power: The Punjab Unionist Party, 1923–1947*. Delhi: Manohar Publishers.

Tutleja, K. L. 1984. *Sikh Politics, 1920–1940*. Kurukshetra: Kurukshetra University Press.

Vaishnav, Milan and Jonathan Guy. 2018. "Does Higher Turnout Hurt Incumbents? An Analysis of State Elections in India', *Studies in Indian Politics*, 6(1): 71–87.

Verma, P. S. 1987. 'The Akali Dal: History, Electoral Performance and Leadership Profile' in Gopal Singh (ed.), *Punjab Today*, New Delhi: Intellectual Publishing House.

Verma, P. S. 1998. 'The Punjab Congress', in J. S. Grewal and Indu Banga (eds.), *Punjab in Prosperity and Violence*. New Delhi: K. K. Publisher, pp. 27–64.

Verma, P. S. 1999. 'Akali-BJP Debacle in Punjab: Wages of Non-Performance and Fragmentation', *Economic and Political Weekly*, December 11.

Wallace, Paul. 2000. 'Electoral Politics in Punjab', in Paul Wallace and Ramashray Roy (eds.), *India's 1999 Elections and 20th Century Politics*. New Delhi: Sage.

Weber, Max. 1978. *Economy and Society: An Outline of Interpretive Sociology*. California: California University Press.

Weiner, Myron. 1967. *Party Building in a New Nation-The Indian National Congress*. Chicago: Chicago University Press.

Weiner, Myron (ed.). 1968. *State Politics in India*. Princeton: Princeton University Press.

Weiner, Myron. 1977. *India at the Polls: The Parliamentary Elections of 1977*. Washington, DC: American Enterprise Institute for Public Policy Research.

Weiner, Myron and John Osgood Field (eds.). 1974. *Electoral Politics in Indian States*, Vol. 1, 2 and 3. New Delhi: Manohar.

Wood, John R. 1984. (ed.). *State Politics in Contemporary India: Crisis or Continuity*. Boulder: Westview Press.

Wyatt, Andrew. 2010. *Party System Change in South India: Political Entrepreneurs*. Patterns and Processes. London: Routledge.

Wyatt, Andrew. 2015a. 'Arvind Kejriwal's Leadership of the Aam Aadmi Party', *Contemporary South Asia*, 23(2): 167–180, www.tandfonline.com/doi/abs/10.1080/09584935.2015.1025038?af=R&journalCode=ccsa20 (accessed full article through the author on 18 May 2019).

Wyatt, Andrew. 2015b. 'India in 2014: Decisive National Elections', *Asian Survey*, 55(1): 33–47, www.academia.edu/11425678/India_in_2014_Decisive_National_Elections (accessed on 16 May 2019).

Yadav, Yogendra. 1992. 'Who Won in Punjab? Of the Real Contest', *Frontline*, 9(7): 12–26.

Yadav, Yogendra. 1996. 'Reconfiguration in Indian Politics: State Assembly Elections, 1993–95', *Economic and Political Weekly*, 34(35): 2393–9.

Yadav, Yogendra. 1999. 'Electoral Politics in the Time of Change: India's Third Electoral System, 1989–99', *Economic and Political Weekly*, XXXIV(35): 2393–9.

Yadav, Yogendra and Suhas Palshikar. 2009a. 'Principal State Level Contests and Derivative National Choices: Electoral Trends in 2004–2009', *Economic and Political Weekly*, February 7: 55–62.

Yadav, Yogendra and Suhas Palshikar. 2009b. 'Ten Theses on State Politics in India', in Sandeep Shastri, K. C. Suri and Yogendra Yadav (eds.), *Electoral Politics in Indian States: Lok Sabha Elections in 2004 and Beyond*. New Delhi: Oxford University Press, pp. 46–63.

Ziegfeld, Adam. 2012. 'Coalition Government and Party System Change: Explaining the Rise of Regional Parties in India', *Comparative Politics*, 45(1): 69–87.

Ziegfeld, Adam. 2016. *Why Regional Parties? Clientelism, Elites, and the Indian Party System*. Cambridge: Cambridge University Press.

Index

Printed in the United States
By Bookmasters